A New Model

A New Model

WHAT CONFIDENCE, BEAUTY, AND POWER REALLY LOOK LIKE

Ashley Graham

with Rebecca Paley

DEY ST.

An Imprint of WILLIAM MORROW

All photographs are courtesy of the author's personal collection.

The names and identifying details of some individuals discussed in this book were changed to protect their privacy.

HarperCollins books may be purchased for educational, business, or sales promotional use. For information, please e-mail the Special Markets Department at SPsales@harpercollins.com.

FIRST EDITION

Designed by Renata De Oliveira

Library of Congress Cataloging-in-Publication Data has been applied for.

ISBN 978-0-06-266794-6
ISBN 978-0-06-274144-8 (Barnes & Noble signed edition)
ISBN 978-0-06-274143-1 (Target signed edition)

17 18 19 20 21   DIX/LSC   10 9 8 7 6 5 4 3 2 1

For Justin

Contents

You are good enough to make whatever you want to achieve possible. You just need to find your talent and passion—then put a heck of a lot of work into it.

Don't fall into the trap of sacrificing your self-esteem for affection and acceptance. No matter what your size, you are a sexy goddess. Remember that.

Every day is a new day and a new struggle. But with a little reflection, you can develop the tools to put that Snickers down or not care so much when you don't want to.

How not to win friends and influence people—or feel good about yourself: over-the-top partying, shopping, paying for others, and sleeping around. Believe me, I tried all of that and more.

Introduction
My (Cellulite) Revolution

I'm in three places at once right now, doing half a dozen different things. Sitting in a director's chair, I'm getting my hair and makeup done—and my picture taken by about a dozen event photographers at the same time. I'm also taking over *Harper's Bazaar*'s Snapchat and *Elle Canada*'s Instagram, so my phone is on fire. In about sixty seconds I'm going to be on the move, making sure that boobs are in the right place and bodysuits don't accidently open, because, while I'm obviously not ashamed of the female form, we don't need a crotch shot on the runway during my show.

Oh, and I'm keeping a smile on my face the whole time. Because if you're awful to someone just once, that means you're awful for the rest of your life.

It might be forgivable if I snapped, since I am very nervous (so nervous I woke up this morning and had to run to the toilet). The show for this year's New York Fashion Week is featuring *my* lingerie collection for Addition Elle. With my name all over it. Last year when we did the show, the response was huge. The image of me coming down the runway in lacy panties, bra, and heels broke the Internet. (Khloé Kardashian reposted it, and for that week, I was one of the most influential images, along with Pope Francis and President Obama. That was beyond.)

Okay, but that was last year, and in fashion, a year is forever. The big question looming over now me is, will I be able to do it again?

I feel a lot of pressure to have everyone and everything look as amazing as last year. I want to make as big an impact as last year (if not bigger), not just because I'm a model and this is my career, but because showing gorgeous, curvy women walk down a runway in sexy lingerie is part of my bigger mission in my industry and in my life—to prove that every body is different *and* beautiful.

This is the generation of body diversity. We are sick of being told by society, by the fashion industry, by Hollywood, that we are too thin, too fat, too flabby, too tall, too small. Being a woman in the United States now almost definitely means hating at least a part of your body, if not all of it. As a woman unafraid of celebrating my thick thighs in public, I've made it my goal to help others embrace, even love themselves, stretch marks and all.

My evolution into an activist for self-love was a gradual process. I trace the very beginnings of it to the start of my career, when I was surprised at how insecure most models acted. Big or small, it didn't matter. I noticed that so many of these women complained about their cellulite popping out or their arms looking big. It was honestly no different than when the tiny, popular cheerleaders at my high school complained, "I'm so fat today." Although it's so commonplace for women to put themselves down, it's also really uncomfortable to be around. If you hear it enough, you start to believe the things that person is telling herself—and even apply it to yourself.

But when we models put down our physical appearance, it's especially sad because we are being paid to look good. If you are cast in a shoot, the theory is that you are the most beautiful woman for this job. So why would you feel any other way about yourself? I've seen it over and over on set, and it's always ugly to watch. I wanted to be appealing—the girl you can trust and really talk to—so I vowed to myself early on that I would *not* belittle myself, no matter what anyone else said to me or how I felt about myself, privately.

I don't know if it's the reason for my career success (I'm sure it's a part of it), but I've achieved more than anyone ever thought possible for a plus-size model. I have appeared on many magazine covers (like the *Sports Illustrated* Swimsuit issue) despite being told I'd never be a cover girl, landed campaigns for major retailers like Levi's and Sephora, and even walked in a fashion show for H&M in Paris. All of that has helped me push against the status quo for beauty within the fashion industry.

Beyond my career, though, I began to realize that when I was positive about myself, it made others feel better about themselves. I started to get a sense of this effect on set, in little reactions from other models, makeup or hair stylists, managers and photographers. Repeatedly, people told me not only how confident they could see I was but also that it was contagious. I loved that idea so much that it became a way of life for me. My mother, assistant, glam squad, and anyone else I spend a lot of time with have to talk positively about themselves, because if they don't, I check them quickly. (My manager, my agent, my assistant, my publicist, and my book publisher are all curvy women: does that make me biased? Or does that just mean we are really the majority?)

The advent of social media allowed me to bring this message to a much bigger audience than those who knew me from catalogs and magazines. What began as something I did to help myself and the women in my life was suddenly transformed into a way of helping women everywhere. Just like I told *Cosmo* when they put me on their cover, "My cellulite is changing someone's life out there."

I've got to be honest, though. Miss Body Positivity didn't wake up the morning of my fashion show feeling so, well, positive. I felt really mad at myself, because the night before I had gone out to the restaurant Tao and ordered the lobster fried rice. I felt like I had to; it was my best friend's birthday. But, lobster fried rice. The night before a lingerie show. Really? That was pushing it, even for me. But, damn. It *was* so good.

Anyway, I couldn't undo what I'd done—and I couldn't go to the gym that morning—so I just did a sprint up a big hill near my house, showered, and prayed. I thanked God for this opportunity and reminded myself that it's not only about me. If I indulged in a bad day by having a pity party about what I ate and was feeling bad enough about myself that it showed when I walked down the runway, I'd be letting down all those women whose lives I said I wanted to change. It's irrational to think that one slip-up the night before could have changed my body in any meaningful way. The problem was in my mind more than anywhere else, and I never want food to take over my world in this way.

So, instead of putting on the yoga pants and cozying up on the couch like I might have wanted to, I threw on a tight Opening Ceremony knit dress that wasn't just smoking hot—it also wouldn't make any lines or indentations on my body that could be seen later on the runway. (This is the kind of thing you have to think about when you are a model and have some meat on your bones—clothes leaving marks.) I put an embellished Sonia Rykiel jean jacket over that, and I thought to myself, I look good. Now I feel good.

If my affirmations didn't really make me feel better, this crowd at my fashion show does. There are some new girls here and a lot of really good friends, like Georgia Pratt, Marquita Pring, Precious Lee, and Tara Lynn. These are some of the top plus-size models in the industry, and if you haven't heard of them already, you need to learn their names. We all have the same message—no matter what your size, you are beautiful—we have just been given different opportunities to share it. We will make the shift in fashion that needs to happen when many voices are heard. One name does not change an industry. It can make a dent, but to continue the change, we need more women speaking their minds and presenting their diversity. It's empowering to know that this group of high-profile women, my people, are here to support me by being in the show.

All the models are having beachy waves put in their hair, and red liner put around their eyes, which I'm starting to have second thoughts about. The head makeup artist described red as "strong, feminine, and unexpected." It's definitely in style this season, which makes it unexpected for my runway, because plus-size models always get the same kind of makeup—safe. We are always made to look pretty, and commercial pretty. There's a saying that plus-size models are unicorns. There is much more variation in terms of acceptable looks when it comes to straight-size models, including such genres as dolls, androgynous, aliens, and bombshells. But as long as, for the most part, they conform to the right measurements (anywhere from five-nine to six-one and a size 2, 4, or 6), they will find work.

Plus-size models need to have an hourglass figure, a flat stomach, a sweet but skinny face, and, up until about 2010, long hair. (I remember the first time a plus-size model got a pixie cut, and it sent shock waves through the industry because no one was ready for it.) In terms of measurements, you have to be at least five-foot-nine, but being over six feet tall is a big no-no. And you have to fit into plus-size sample sizes, which are 12, 14, and 16. (Smaller models, who are more size 10, have custom bodysuits with padding that fills them out in the breasts, butt, and hips—kind of a reverse Spanx—that they have to carry with them to all their jobs like hair extensions.)

You also hardly ever see plus-size models in high-end fashion magazines, but I'm pushing that envelope too! They don't give the curvy girls the weird, interesting stuff. That's why I initially loved that the makeup team for this show were going in a different, edgier direction. But as the head makeup artist applies the red liner around my eyes, I start to look as if I have a wicked case of pinkeye. . . .

Not a good look for the runway.

I'm committed to the idea that curvy girls can push fashion. We're already doing it. Earlier that week, I went to Christian Siriano's runway show, where he featured five plus-size models. Siriano, a *Project Runway* alum, also does a line for plus-size retailer Lane Bryant, but this show was for his personal line. I love that he's willing to take this stand where many of his peers haven't.

None of this is easy, though. Not even women as gorgeous as the models surrounding me backstage at my lingerie show are immune to feelings of insecurity and even self-hatred. One of the girls (models often affectionately call each other "girls") told me point-blank that if she had to wear a bra and panty set, she wasn't walking. It wasn't a diva moment. "I don't want my stomach jiggling as I go down the runway," she said. And this is a *goddess*. So I gave her a bodysuit to wear.

There is so much anxiety around weight for all women. While I've had moments where I felt really fat (because I've failed to hit the gym for months or have eaten pasta and pizza five nights in a row), for the most part I don't worry about the number on the scale. Don't get me wrong. I have those days where I think I'm the ugliest person alive, but it always stems from a professional failure, like not being able to land the beauty shot a photographer wanted. It's funny that the thing I'm known for—my size—is not something I'm naturally focused on.

It's not that I'm more evolved. I think I'm just missing a certain self-conscious gene. For instance, I have no problem standing around naked right now in front of dozens of hair and makeup people, production assistants, and security guards. That's one of the things Cary, the show's stylist, loves about me. (No shrinking violet himself, Cary is racing around backstage in a mesh tank top that shows full nip, thick gold chains, big hoop earrings, and mirrored sunglasses with gold monkeys sitting atop the frames.) "Let's keep it PG," he says, putting a trench coat on a model whose panties show her entire backside.

Cary and I work together a lot, and he knows that when we're on set, I pretty much have an open door, or open robe, policy. Whereas a lot of models are extremely shy about being naked in front of others, I couldn't care less. In fact, I can't stand changing tents. (These are tents the size of a dressing room stall at a department store that pop up and down for privacy when a model is changing on an outdoor set.) My attitude is, we're here to work, so let's just get it done. I'm not going to take ten minutes to walk over to some change tent when time on a job is so precious. (Unless there are paparazzi—then I have to change in one.) Cary thinks that's me being "body-confident," as he calls it. He describes me as "very free" and says the fact that I'm happy with who I am is the best way for me to relay my message of positivity to others. But the truth is, I'm not thinking about it at all when I strip down in front of tons of people. I just want to do my job!

My whole childhood, I ran around half-naked. So did my little sisters, Madison and Abigail. As the oldest and bossiest, I might have exerted some influence over them. Whatever the reason, the three of us never had much on, even when we became teenagers. We thought it was totally normal to hang around the house in bras and panties.

This is particularly ironic since my mom was *never* naked. (I didn't see my mom's breasts until three years ago, when we were in a hotel room and someone started banging on the door, which I'd forgotten to lock. She jumped out of bed and grabbed her shirt, and I got a full view. "I've never seen your boobs!" I shrieked. She was mortified.)

My mom's prudishness has a lot to do with her growing up Mennonite. She didn't wear a bonnet and *Little House on the Prairie* dresses, but she definitely stayed covered. They were farmers, which is hard, *hard* work. Mom never got to go trick-or-treating on Halloween, because that was harvest time and took priority over all else. Even as a college student, she dropped everything at school to help her parents when they needed it.

Her efforts always met with praise from my grandparents. They expressed gratitude for her willingness to pitch in and never took her hard work for granted. As my mom says,

"I always felt love and acceptance. It didn't matter what I looked like, how big I was, how small I was. That had nothing to do with it. Hard work won praise."

So my mom grew up to be just like her parents. She isn't known for her looks (although she is a very striking, five-foot-eleven blonde). Instead it's her cooking, her hospitality, her unbelievable work ethic, and her relentless positive attitude that make her who she is. These qualities, ingrained in her by her parents' example, defined my childhood, too.

Just as her parents instilled their values in her, so she handed them down to my sisters and me. Having grown up feeling loved and accepted for who she is, my mom conveyed that to her children. (Although she's still uncomfortable with her daughters' habit of going around without clothes. "Where do I look?" she asks me when I talk to her while completely naked, which I do often. "Put something on so I can hear you.")

Although I'm a model and make a living off my looks, my mom always reminded me of all of her inherited values— the first being that looks don't matter. They certainly don't make me more important than anyone else. Mom often said to me, "I know if you look good, you get special treatment." And then she went a step further: "I don't care what the world says or does. You have to remember that every person is valuable."

When I first started traveling to New York to work as a model, at the age of twelve, my mom disregarded all the stereotypes you hear about the Big Apple. Even as a Midwestern, churchgoing farmer's daughter, she didn't approach the city as some kind of den of sin filled with people waiting to take advantage of a naive young girl. Whenever the two of us went to New York, my mom, who at that point always traveled with me when I went on jobs, encouraged me to approach this new and crazy place with a completely open heart.

"Do not hesitate to ask for help," she said. "Look people in the eye when you talk to them. Always look them in the eye. And smile."

"But Mom, you're not supposed to look at people in New York! Everybody knows that. I'll get sold into prostitution or something."

"That's baloney," she said. "People are nice. You look at people and you smile, odds are you're going to get a smile back."

It's true! Even in New York City.

That's not all. After my modeling career took off and I moved to Manhattan full-time, my mom continued to remind me to be nice. When I eventually wound up living in a doorman building in the Financial District, my mom said, "Find out your doorman's name, so that when you're walking in you can always say hello to him by name." There was a laundry at the base of the building where I took my clothes, and again, Mom said, "Find out the names of the ladies who do your washing, and tell them you appreciate it. They work as hard as you do, if not harder. And they deserve the same respect that you are getting."

Love your neighbor as yourself. Even when you're living in Lower Manhattan.

Mom was right. I internalized her advice of being kind to others, not just because it's the right way to live but because it also made my life better. And I attribute my career success in no small part to following my mom's example. Even in an industry as catty and competitive as modeling can be, you get nothing by thinking you are better than everyone.

That's why at my lingerie show, when the lead hairstylist asks me if I want a side part (how I usually wear my hair) or a center part like the rest of the girls, I say, "I want to look like everyone else."

"How long do you want it?" asks the hairstylist, taking out a huge bag of hair extensions.

"How long is everyone else doing it?"

"To the bra strap."

"So there."

I go through the same thing with the manicurist, who wants to know if I'm also getting a charcoal-gray on my nails.

"Yes, I'm like every other girl."

Even when I get demanding, I do it with kindness. As it turns out, the red eyeliner isn't chic; it's hideous. When the makeup artist at first shows me my face in the mirror, I try to be cool: "It looks weird. . . ." I try to convince myself it looks cool. But I just can't. I hate it. I understand Addition Elle is being fashion forward, which I love, but I don't feel comfortable with this look on me. So, I don't ask, I tell the team that we are changing up the makeup (red only on the bottom, thinner and smudgier.) Although it's a command, I deliver it in a unique way that my husband, Justin, has pointed out.

Basically I explode into this huge, maniacal laugh at the end of my bidding that makes the other person start laughing with me, so that before they know it they're saying yes to whatever I've asked, which in this case happens to be a complete makeup change about an hour before my show. "We're changing the makeup. *Mwa ha, ha, ha, ha.*"

And the makeup artist is so cool about it, especially considering that the last hour before a runway show is where it *really* gets crazy (the last fifteen minutes are pure chaos)—and of course that's exactly when Mom arrives with her best friend, whom I call Aunt Barb. They are wearing all black like I instructed.

I know she's there before I can see her. Her voice booms, "Hi!" And that huge laugh? Guess where I inherited it from. We are a loud family.

With three different people working curling irons on my extensions, the manicurist painting my toes, and a fashion reporter asking me questions, my mom says, "I want a photo with you." She is a mom, after all.

After I give her a few eye rolls (I am her daughter, after all), Mom and Barb disappear, and suddenly it's crunch time.

2:44 p.m. I'm getting my legs oiled up by two people, with another putting powder on my décolletage and to cover up a bruise on my leg.

3:06 p.m. The dressers spring into action and the girls line up! "Make sure the bra is on the tightest setting," I shout. "And the swell of the breast is in the right place!"

3:15 p.m. For the first time all day, it's totally quiet behind stage. The show starts. I really, really have to pee, but I ignore it.

And no more than ten minutes later, it's all over. Five hours of prep, weeks of worry, months of designing, and in less time than a techno song, it's all done.

Buzzing with adrenaline, I feel like I killed it. But did I? I need to see a photo, because I know what's going to happen. Everybody's going to compare my body to last year, talk about whether it looks good or not good, if I'm fatter or skinnier. I can already see all the articles and blog posts debating the finer points of my thighs. Who cares? I try to tell myself. In the same moment, though, I'm overwhelmed with the insecurity that every woman feels when she puts herself out there—whether it is on the runway, walking down the aisle at her wedding, at the beach, or on a first date.

Did I look good?

I wish my question were different, but it is what it is. I don't possess some superhuman quality that makes me impervious to criticism and negativity. There are always going to be people who make you feel bad about yourself. (Just the other day on a set, someone asked me how old I was, and when I answered, "Twenty-nine," this person responded, "I guess you're not just about body diversity but age diversity, too." Ouch!) It's not about your size—or your age—but how you carry yourself and how you handle situations that sometimes aren't fair.

Vulnerability isn't a sin, and everyone is entitled to his or her feelings. But I'm here to tell you that although I didn't start out liking my cellulite or stretch marks (and I don't always appreciate them to this day), I faked it until eventually it felt real. It's just like when you put yourself down so often you begin to internalize the criticisms—if you act like you're amazing, you begin to believe it.

As if she can read my mind, my publicist approaches, holding her phone up to my face. She's got the photo up: me, facing the world in a bra and panties, confident and strong.

Yeah, I slayed.

A New
Model

chapter 1

Fame, Fortune, Self-Love—

What Modeling Doesn't Get You

You are good enough to make whatever you want to achieve possible. You just need to find your talent and passion—then put a heck of a lot of work into it.

One of the questions I get all the time from young women is, "How do I become a model?"

I never answer that question. There are plenty of agents, books, and other sources better equipped to give professional advice than me. Instead I pose my own question.

"Let me ask you this: Do you want to become a model because it's going to make you feel pretty, earn a lot of money, or become famous?"

And here comes the hard truth.

"Because, if so, none of that is going to happen."

I know that must seem like a real load of BS coming from me, or even cruel. I've been lucky, because becoming a model has given me all those things and more than I've ever imagined. But fame, in my case and in pretty much all cases, is pure luck (not to mention a ton of hard work). It just is. If there were a formula to it, a lot more people would be famous. Most models who work consistently do so in complete obscurity, like any other job. It is a select few who become household names in the modeling world. A very select few.

And the money thing? You can definitely make a lot of money—if you're the "it" girl, which is as rare as making it as an actress or pop musician. (If you *are* the "it" girl, you'd better know how to invest your money, because you won't be the "it" girl for long—more on that later.) The rates for magazine work and fashion shows are much less than people imagine, and a lot of a model's time is taken up not with paying jobs but with going from casting to casting, where the competition is so fierce that she's much more likely to be rejected than hired.

Last up: the pretty thing. No matter how many hairstylists, makeup artists, fashion stylists, and Photoshop experts you employ, being a model makes you feel seriously ugly. Because your appearance is your profession, it's also fair game for criticism. When you're a model, people pick apart and manipulate every single aspect of your exterior. No part of you is off limits.

I give that hard-truth talk to all aspiring models, because although I want them to know what they are getting into, I understand the drive behind the desire.

Before I even turned "pretty," I sought out the limelight. Heck, before I could eat solid food I was an attention hog, according to my mother. Apparently, I was "colorful" (my mom's word) even as an infant. When she would lay me on a blanket on the floor, I would lift up my head and look around the room with "presence" (again, my mom). I always looked people in the eye, even as a two-year-old when we went to Disney World and I decided to say hi to everyone I passed. By three years old, I took to standing behind the pulpit in church to give a sermon to an empty sanctuary. Yeah, I was very comfortable with myself. And no stage was too small for me. I also used the fireplace hearth as a podium for my greatness.

When my younger sisters, Maddie and Abby, came into the picture, I included them in *my* show. I didn't mind sharing the limelight as long as I was the loudest and most memorable. We danced and sang. Every Christmas, we put on a whole talent show for our family. No matter the occasion, I was the director *and* the star.

We moved around a lot when I was growing up, because of my dad's job in database marketing. I was only a month or two old when we moved to Atlanta, where we lived until I was four years old. Mom was eight months pregnant with Madison when we moved to New Hampshire and seven months pregnant with Abby when we moved to Conway, Arkansas. So, with some combination of infants, toddlers, and pregnancy, my mom, a homemaker, landed in new houses in unfamiliar towns where she didn't know a soul. On top of that, my dad traveled so much for work, she was usually alone at home with my sisters and me.

Now that I'm grown up, I can't even fathom what my mom went through. I have a panic attack if Seamless isn't working right. I can't imagine cooking for a family of five every night. But whether it was in Arkansas, New Hampshire, or, later, Dallas and then back to Nebraska, she always created a homey home, filled with people, food, and fun. She made friends with the neighbors or through church, and she was always cooking. Mom wanted the house full. She loved noise, talking, laughter, and music. Our record player was always playing Amy Grant or Shania Twain. My sisters and I would come up with dance routines to the songs that we presented to my mom as if it were a real show. She loved it.

It wasn't until I became an adult that I learned my mother had never wanted to move to all these different towns. She confided in me recently how hard it was for her to build relationships and regimens, only to have them vanish into thin air as soon as it was time for us to move on to the next place. Despite the loss of friendships and the fear of finding new ones wherever we were headed, Mom always portrayed moving as a great adventure. "You're going to meet your newest best friend," she would tell my sisters and me. "She is waiting to meet you at the next stop."

"Yay!" we shouted, jumping up and down. She made moving exciting for us, even though inside she was grieving.

Many people who moved around a lot as kids talk about how horrible the experience was. I never felt anxious or sad, and that's thanks to my mother's constant presence. It makes sense to me now that I didn't worry about leaving behind friends, schools, or bedrooms, because I had my mom. She was always there and always nurturing, though not in a "there, there" after you've fallen way. She didn't care at all if you fell; one time I lay in the street for a good five minutes after a nasty fall from my bicycle, crying or pretending to, and waiting for Mom to come running out of the house with a warm compress or something. But she didn't, so I just stood up and dusted myself off. That was what she wanted for us—to get up and go, no matter what happened. "What are we gonna do today?" was her mantra. "Let's have fun!"

It wasn't until we moved to Nebraska when I was twelve that I considered modeling. Before then people told me I was pretty, but when we lived in Texas, I remember thinking, "I'm not *that* pretty."

The reason I thought that had nothing to do with the fact that I wore glasses or was already developing a curvy woman's body. It was because I wasn't really popular. Like so many other young women, I equated popularity with beauty. In Dallas, the rich girls with the blondest, shiniest hair, best clothes, and skinniest bodies—*they* were highest on the social ladder. Not a loudmouth, dark-haired chick with the boobs, hips, and thighs of a twenty-five-year-old.

So, after we moved to Nebraska, when I was approached by someone from a modeling agency while at the mall with my dad, I was surprised. I was only twelve years old, but I was pretty sure I already knew how I rated. The man presented himself in that friendly, frank, Midwestern way, saying his name was Clark, he was from I & I, an agency out of Kansas City, Missouri, and that he would love to talk to me about being a model.

Clark wasn't creepy in the least, in part because what he was proposing was a series of classes that cost almost two thousand dollars. At the end of the program I would have a portfolio and a chance to meet representatives from bigger agencies at a modeling convention.

A day later my parents and I were mulling over a packet of information with an overview of I & I's program in a hotel convention hall. One thing that was clear to everyone present: this was an expensive proposition. Still, many were willing to pay it.

"Look, we are making a sacrifice," my dad said to me, "because this seems to be something you really want."

My dad was always telling me that he wanted me to be enthusiastic about something. Although my parents were both college athletes, I wasn't into sports like my little sisters. And, although I liked to be in the spotlight, I didn't like acting. Other than getting the part of C-3PO (because of my height) for a stage version of *Star Wars,* I wasn't part of the drama clique at school. I wasn't enthusiastic about academics. Not at all. After being diagnosed with dyslexia in the fourth grade (the same year I had to get glasses), I was in special classes and had tutors for the rest of my school years, but schoolwork never got any easier. Instead of putting ten times more into mastering what other kids could do easily, I focused on charming my teachers, which worked to get me passing grades but didn't result in my actually learning much of anything.

Modeling was the first thing I was really, truly "into." My mom was just as into it, and she was excited for me. Although she doesn't understand high-end fashion (like I still sometimes don't), she loves clothes. My mom, who likes to say, "It's always better to be overdressed than underdressed," wears full makeup every day and goes shopping almost every week. She isn't extravagant about it, though. My grandma—who was extremely beautiful as a young woman—didn't spend a lot of money on her appearance but still managed to put herself together well. My mom is the same way.

Although modeling sounded like a fun dress-up party, my mom approached the opportunity before me no differently than she would have if I had taken a part-time job or joined a sports team. Because she grew up in a family where the only yardstick anyone was measured by had to do with how hard you were willing to work, that's how I would be judged as a model. To her, my success had less to do with how pretty I was and more to do with the effort I put into it.

None of this was lost on me as I signed up for I & I's program that day in the convention hotel room. My mom and dad were spending all this money to make an investment in me. There was no way I was going to disappoint them.

The modeling course was a big deal. My mom spent so much time driving me three hours each way to Kansas City for all-day conventions, where I learned the basics of modeling, such as what goes in a professional portfolio; how to act in a casting session, including shaking everybody's hand and looking people in the eye; and how to walk down a runway. One teacher showed us how to create different expressions for the camera while another instructed us on what to have in our model bag. At the level of modeling we aspired to—catalog work for regional department stores like Gordmans—you needed to bring a bag with your own shoes, undergarments, and deodorant. (Sometimes you needed to show up with your hair and makeup already done, as well.) I used my dad's sea-green overnight bag to haul around a pair of brown and black heels, brown and black boots, and sneakers—just in case. It was a very large bag.

I & I wasn't promising its students the cover of *Vogue* or even regional catalog work, but the school pledged to teach us everything we needed to know in order to walk, talk, and act like a model. I soaked up every second of the course as if I were learning the meaning of life. It was totally obvious to everyone, out of the group of thirty young men and women in my program, that very few of us, if any, were actually going to become working models. There were some who enrolled simply to build their self-confidence and self-esteem. Like the old ad campaign for some modeling school used to say, "Train like a model or just look like one." But I listened diligently to every single word those teachers said. Whether it was learning how to hold my head or half-close my eyes or the best kind of shoes to put in my modeling bag, the information provided me with a framework for my fantasies and desires, a way to better myself and put effort toward a set of concrete goals. I had something to be enthusiastic about.

Six months after I started the program, I had the first true test of my abilities. The culmination of the course was to be a massive modeling expo held in Texas. During the two-day event, the thirty of us were going to run through a series of exercises, such as a runway show and a big group dance number to exhibit rhythm and technique—all of which are essential to modeling, where you have to know how to move your body.

Representatives from all the big modeling agencies, like Ford and Wilhelmina, were present to see if there were any fresh faces they liked. Signing with one of these power players was the true goal of the convention. As I went around shaking the hands of all the New York City folks, looking them in the eye as I had been trained, I experienced the self-consciousness of being on display. But I didn't feel pressure.

Part of my ease stemmed from the fact that my mom and dad, while making sure I understood the significance of the money they had spent on modeling school, didn't expect me to turn the experience into a full-blown career. Even though I struggled in school because of learning disabilities and lack of interest, my mom and dad assumed that I was going to college. That was their number one goal—not my becoming a model. So they took a very laid-back, let's-see-what-happens approach to the whole thing. My mom summed it up when she said, "Are you pretty? We don't know."

She didn't question my prettiness to be hurtful, and I wasn't hurt by her comment. I know my mom loves me and thinks I'm beautiful. That's just my mom. We have very similar personalities in that we always say what's on our mind. She was just as curious as I was whether *other* people in the fashion industry would consider me modelworthy.

The other reason I was kind of cool about the New York modeling agencies at the convention was that I had already done my first real-life modeling job by this point! Like they did with all their students, I & I sent my photo to local retailers as a "new model on the market," and Pamida, a Midwestern department store chain, wanted me because I lived only an hour's drive away (and I guess they liked the way I looked).

Even though I was just twelve years old, my first job was a print ad for a retailer—with me wearing a see-through bra. You read that right! Now, I didn't know that before I booked the job, and neither did my mom. She and I prayed before we went in for the shoot. "God, if this is the only job that Ashley gets, we are so grateful," she said.

"Yes," I added. "I'm just so happy, Lord, that you blessed me with this one modeling job."

I *was* happy. With my modeling bag, complete with shoes and deodorant, I might as well have been walking onto the set of a *Vogue* shoot. Except that I had to do my own hair and makeup. I never really could really figure out how to do my hair, because my mom had never been able to do it. Its texture was so different from hers. She had fine, feather-straight hair while I have thick curls that my mom would always brush through and make really puffy, causing us to fight every morning. Eventually I told my mom I just wanted to cut it all off, which I did—into a horrible bowl cut. (To this day I don't know how to do my own hair. Thank God, I have people for that.)

To prepare for my first photo shoot, I actually took a clothes iron to it in order to keep it straight. The people at Pamida definitely had to touch up my idea of perfect hair and makeup when I walked in. The stylist then said, "Okay, we have one bra for you to do." I put it on, and there were my breasts, already huge and on full display in a size 36C under a thin layer of see-through mesh. My mom was calm throughout the whole shoot, but she did ask to sign a piece of paper that promised Pamida would airbrush my nipples out of the final ad—and next thing you know, the shoot was over and I was on my way.

I loved it.

Not only did I have the photographer, art director, and stylist telling me I was beautiful, they also told me how great I moved in front of the camera. The photographer even asked me if I had taken dance classes, because "you know your body so well." I hadn't; I've just always been comfortable in front of the camera. As early as two years old, I would look into the video camera and say, "Mom, are you filming me?" It was a demand, not a question. It was the personality I was born with. Modeling offered a new exciting venue for me that none of my friends or anyone I knew had ever had. Plus, I got paid three hundred dollars! It was a win, win, win.

The bra shoot gave me a huge boost of confidence as I went into the two-day convention in Texas, where people congratulated me for already having done a job. Because nobody else had booked a job, I felt I had a leg up. The result was that I felt like the pressure was off a little bit. I spent those two days having a lot of fun and won the award for top plus-size model. (My mom still has the trophy.) More important, though, Wilhelmina called my house the next day with the news: they wanted to sign me!

My mom, dad, and I were now off to New York City, the fashion capital of the world! I was thirteen years old.

Cue the cheesy soundtrack music to a montage of touristy images from our trip to the Big Apple. We stayed at the Empire Hotel, looking over the glimmering golden lights of Lincoln Center on the Upper West Side, and went to Times Square, where we visited such centers of culture as Madame Tussauds wax museum.

As soon as the three of us walked into Wilhelmina's offices, the cheesy music came to a screeching halt. Seriously, the place was dead quiet. All you could hear was the sound of typing; everyone was staring at a computer screen. Some looked up at us for a second and then went right back to typing. Even if they knew who we were, they wouldn't act like it. These were fashion people. We definitely weren't in Nebraska anymore. It was very intimidating, to say the least.

After walking for what seemed like a mile, we arrived at a large front desk and announced who we were. The pretty young woman behind the desk hit a few buttons on her phone.

"Ashley Graham's here to see you," she said in a monotone that showed she couldn't have cared less who I was.

We stood there waiting for a few awkward moments until another pretty young woman arrived and wordlessly walked us through a huge, open room divided by half walls covered with images of different models' faces. Each section was devoted to a different part of Wilhelmina's business: men, kids, catalog, high-end, editorial—and then plus size. That section was all the way in the back. As soon as we got to it, I saw my photo. That moment was so surreal. To see my picture up on this wall, with all these other girls, beautiful women who lived glamorous, independent lives having people do their hair and makeup . . .

"Hello," a short, unsmiling blonde said. This was my new agent, Amanda. Everything about her was immediately intimidating: her fast-talking, no-nonsense approach, her direct gaze. She was what people would call a quintessential New Yorker, and she got to the point right away. "We have to get you in front of everyone," she said. "It's casting time. I hope you're ready."

Modeling and fashion are *very* serious. As a model, you can't make jokes. At the same time, though, you have to show you have personality. It sounds like a cliché, but there's more to it than just being a pretty face. You have to fit right in this very narrow zone where you have personality but not *too* much personality. You need to talk, because if you don't talk at all, you're a depressing model. But if you talk too much, then you're a know-it-all. It's like that with everything: smiling, laughing, giving ideas, having a point of view. Have some, do some, be some . . . but not too much.

My practice in charming my teachers at school was good training for modeling. This was an evolving process, but I made it my mission to become friends with my agents. I made sure they knew me in and out, so when they called clients about me, they were not only excited to pitch me but also had real specifics on why I would be good for that particular brand.

Although I was young, I understood there were unspoken rules to being successful in the industry. One of them is that you have to be ready to do anything. I am that girl, ready for a challenge, who always says yes. That includes acting like a fool in front of anyone and everyone. When a photographer told me, "Now dance!" even though there was no music, and I had the client, makeup and hair stylists, and about six other people staring at me, I danced. Instead of worrying about looking like an idiot, I just went for it. No matter what the test, you have to try, because even in failing you are eventually going to succeed. With every experience, even ones where you look like a goof or mess up, you are growing. That's why I always ask for constructive criticism from my team, which now includes my agent, publicist, and manager. It doesn't matter if I've given a speech or shot a bathing suit catalog, I will always ask my team, "What could I do better?" There's always room for growth.

When I was first starting out in my career, my goal was to make it, not necessarily to the top, but far enough to afford to live on what I made as a model. I didn't even know what "the top" was back then. I certainly had no idea who the really big plus-size models were at that time, like Kate Dillon or Emme. I had only really heard about Cindy Crawford, and only because people sometimes compared me to her. Once when it happened, I told my dad.

"Someone said I look like Cindy Crawford," I said.

"I wouldn't tell people that," he said. "It sounds like you're bragging."

Constant criticism—that was my dad through and through.

Dad came on that first trip to New York, but when I started working regularly, it was my mom who always traveled with me. He wasn't a regular presence at home, either, since he was usually away traveling for business. But when he was home, he was a dark presence, the polar opposite of my mom. He always seemed to be angry. The house wasn't clean enough or there wasn't food on the table for him to eat. He'd get mad if we were loud. We were three girls; of course we were going to be loud.

We had the Fear of Dad in us, because when he got mad we knew there would be consequences—yelling and maybe even spanking (both parents spanked us). He never hit us hard, but he was like most old-school southern parents. Wooden spoons were weapons; belts could be used, too, in extreme cases.

His insults, though, hurt way more than any of his slaps, and my father was a master of the cutting insult. His nickname for me was "Duh," because he didn't think I was very smart. It wasn't just that I didn't do well in school. I also have a tendency to say whatever comes to my mind—a family trait—and they aren't always the most brilliant insights, particularly some of those I came up with as a little kid. For example, when I was about eight years old, we drove by a church with a big sign that read, "First Baptist Church." From the backseat, I asked, "Is that the first Baptist church, ever?"

"Duh!" my dad said.

His opinion of my intelligence didn't improve much as I got older. During a parent-teacher conference, my eighth-grade social studies teacher spoke to my parents about my common sense (or lack thereof). My dad was the one who used the term *common sense,* but what they were really talking about was my trouble keeping up with my academic work and the fact that I was a social butterfly, who constantly had to be told to stop talking in class. Instead of asking for strategies that I could follow to improve, my dad just dismissed the teacher's concerns. He chalked it up to my lack of intelligence and "common sense." Like he said to me when he got home from the meeting, "I told your teacher, 'If there were a fire, Ashley would start putting on makeup and doing her hair in preparation for the arrival of the firemen.'"

My mom always acted as a buffer between Dad and us girls. If he was mad at us, she tried her best to take the brunt of it so that we wouldn't have to. When he did lash out at us, she defended his actions as best she could. "Your dad does it because he loves you and only wants the best for you."

I didn't doubt my mother's words, but that my dad

thought being mean was the best thing for my sisters and me (since he treated us all the same way) made it hurt even more.

Fashion is a harsh industry, and I learned this from the very start. This is why, whenever aspiring models ask me for advice, I don't sugarcoat the scrutiny they'll come under. I've had agents, casting directors, and so many others pick me apart from head to toe. But the worst I ever felt in my entire career was when, a few years into my career, my dad agreed with my new agent, who said I needed to "tighten up." (By this time I had left Wilhelmina and moved to Ford, where I would be for ten years.)

When I told him what the agent said—that if I wanted to "make it big" I should take off the weight I had been continuously gaining every year since I was discovered at twelve—my dad replied, "Yeah, well, then you need to do it." Riding in the backseat of a taxi with my mother, I cried—not because I didn't get a particular job or because someone in the profession had said something negative about me. No, I was sobbing because my dad thought I should lose weight.

The truth is, I never knew what my weight was. As a model, you don't have to weigh yourself, because you can't see weight, and a model's job is to fit into clothes. Meaning, if you're six feet tall and 200 pounds, you are a size 12, but if you're five-eight and 200 pounds, you are a 16. That's why measurements are the true "measure" of a model's size. If your hips are 40 inches, you are generally a size 10. Hips 42, size 12. Hips 44, size 14. And so on. For that reason, I have never had a scale in my apartment. The only way I know my weight is from going to the doctor's office. (That's how I know that when I got married, I was at the heaviest I've ever been: 215 pounds and a size 16–18. My skinniest ever was 150 pounds and a size 12—when I was twelve years old.) From the time I was discovered in Nebraska, I continued to grow consistently each year so that by the time I graduated from high school, I was a full size 14 and definitely on track toward 16.

After my agent's comment I attempted a teenager's idea of a diet, but I have the kind of body (or mind) that makes me just gain weight if I try to diet. Growing and changing so quickly, it was just impossible for me to lose weight. I don't know if it was hunger or hormones or just hatred for my dad, but in that cab racing up the West Side Highway, I was over-whelmed with emotion. "Your dad loves you," my mom said, stroking my hair. "He really does—he's looking at it from a business standpoint."

I didn't doubt that Dad loved me, and of course my sisters and I loved him. He was handsome, tall, athletic, cool, he took care of us. But nobody ever wanted to be alone with him. It wasn't because we were scared of him. Despite his bad temper, he never stepped over the line. No, we were just uncomfortable around him. It was so bad that over the next couple of years, as I traveled more and more for work, I never wanted my dad to drive me to the airport. Being trapped alone in a car with him for an hour was just hell. I didn't want to say anything to him for fear of inviting one of his digs or barbs.

My first trip to New York to meet Amanda at Wilhelmina set the tone for the next several years. I started working right away. My first booking came on that very first trip. It was an amazing one, too. I became the first plus-size girl for Jennifer Lopez's clothing line JLO. That job was the gig that kept on giving. Andy Hilfiger, Tommy Hilfiger's brother and the fashion exec who helped launch the brand, sent me loads of the clothes after the shoot. It was fun to receive huge boxes filled with those classic JLO looks from the early 2000s, the velour jumpsuits, plunging bodysuits, all booty-hugging.

I thought baggy clothes were ugly on me and that when I wore tight clothes I looked skinnier. Plus, I loved to show my breasts, even though my mom would say to me, "If it's not for sale, don't sell it." (My answer to her was to shake my boobs in her face and say, "Maybe it is for sale." She just rolled her eyes and let me be me.) If there is something about you that you like, show it off—that's my motto. If you think you look good, others will, too. When I was an adolescent, though, I couldn't wear the popular body-conscious teen styles from Abercrombie & Fitch or American Eagle, because they didn't make clothes in my size. On the rare occasion I found something that worked, I always bought it in three colors.

That's why I was so psyched when I received all those JLO clothes; not only did they fit me but they were also my style! Those outfits definitely caught people's attention in Nebraska, where folks weren't hip to sexy, Miami-inspired style. Some kids made fun of me in my big hoop earrings and belly shirts. Those who didn't got a lot of free clothes. I loved sharing the bounty with my friends. Just recently, a girl I had given clothes to commented on my Facebook page that she remembered getting those clothes from me but that she didn't have the courage to wear them until she saw me and my big velour-swathed butt. I'm so grateful for the generosity shown me by Andy—whom I still run into occasionally—he was so generous.

At the JLO casting, I was asked, "Will you raise up your shirt?" I had to show my stomach to prove that it was flat and smooth. And that's how I got the job—because not only did I have brown hair and a sweet face but also a flat, olive-skinned stomach. I've never done much in the way of stomach exercises. It's simply genetic. My mom still has a flat stomach after giving birth to three children. (What I have is a wide, square butt.)

The combination of attributes that landed me the JLO job is what kept me working consistently through my high school years. For plus-size models, if you can't do lingerie and swimwear, you aren't going to make as much money. The flat stomach is key. Because I had a flat stomach, a lot of people wanted me for lingerie and swimwear shoots. And because my face is approachable, I appear racially ambiguous, my body is proportionate, and I can fit into sample sizes, which for the plus-size industry are 12, 14, and 16.

I booked a lot of catalog jobs—both for swimsuits and

lingerie, as well as retailers such as Nordstrom, Dillard's, and Macy's. The fact that I could do both of those meant that I always had plenty of work. Catalog jobs are good money. They don't give you as much money or exposure as campaigns for such brands as Tiffany's, Clinique, or Louis Vuitton, but they are much more consistent. Catalog work certainly pays a lot more than editorial (which means appearing in fashion magazines such as *Vogue* or *Glamour*). Those jobs offer a lot of exposure but very little money. Plus-size models didn't get many campaigns or editorial jobs—if any. And the catalog work when I started out didn't have nearly the scope it does toady. Many more opportunities exist because of new brands devoted to curvy customers and department stores and retailers that have added plus-size divisions.

Still, when I moved to my new agent at Ford, I was working so much, I became known as a "cash cow." Believe it or not, that was a big compliment.

Long before I graduated from high school, I was traveling at least once a month to New York, Germany, or Dallas for work. During those years I became very good friends with Crystal Renn, who at the time was probably the most successful plus-size model. Her story is pretty well known now, but at the time it was a very big deal. Basically, the raven-haired beauty was discovered by a modeling scout who told her she could have a career if she lost weight. By the time she was fifteen and had moved to New York to be a professional model, she had lost more than 42 percent of her original body weight through diuretics, Diet Coke, extreme exercise, and sugar-free gum. Weighing ninety-five pounds, she had shrunk her hip size from 43 inches to 34. But she couldn't maintain that way of living, or that weight. Her body began to rebel, and then so did she. When her former agency told her she had to lose weight, she refused, started to eat, and signed with Ford. When she returned to the industry, she blew up—in a good way. Her career skyrocketed as she landed editorial spreads in *Vogue, Glamour,* and *Harper's Bazaar,* as well as many high-fashion campaigns for brands like Dolce & Gabbana.

Although she was only a year and a half older (she was seventeen and I was sixteen when we met and became friends), Crystal was my mentor. She took me under her wing and showed me the lay of the land of modeling.

We met at Ford right after I signed, and I was instantly mesmerized by her. With her long, raven hair, cool fashion sense, and laid-back demeanor, Crystal was unlike any girl I'd ever met before. After looking me up and down, she said in her very chill way, "I like you."

Wow, I thought, this chick is interesting.

At that time, plus-size models were generally pretty in a wholesome way, definitely not edgy in the way Crystal was. The conventional wisdom was that you couldn't work as an edgy plus-size model. She was the one who singlehandedly changed that preconceived notion.

But we bonded over more ordinary things, like the fact that both of us had been raised Christian and were still virgins. Later, when I moved to New York full-time, Crystal became my everything—first and best friend, the person I could do anything with and tell anything to. Crystal and I hung out morning, noon, and night. We smoked cigarettes, but we didn't get into trouble, because she wasn't a party girl. Mostly, we spent our time focused on our main passion: modeling.

Crystal really taught me how to model. She and I would spend all our time in her apartment, where she had this huge, full-length mirror and a massive stack of *Vogue*s (at this point in my life I was like, "What's *Vogue*?").

"Okay," my model mentor would say, smoothing out one of the fashion spreads. Crystal picked a picture and told me to mimic it for the mirror.

We spent hours in front of that mirror, a stand-in for the camera, flipping the hair, twisting our bodies, changing facial expressions through eyebrows, mouth, or chin—and then doing them all at once. We modeled together or took turns snapping pictures of each other. It was so much fun. We didn't just "work" but also spent a ton of time gossiping. Some of it was pure drama (what were the other girls in our division at the agency up to?) and some of it was serious—like her fraught relationship with her mom and mine with my dad. As I said, when I moved to New York, Crystal was my everything.

By the time my parents and I had a serious discussion about me moving to New York, I was so ready. I had already been traveling on my own for a year. My mom started to let me do that when I was sixteen, but she began prepping me to be independent as soon as I signed with Wilhelmina. Even as a twelve-year-old, there was talk from my agents and parents about my moving to New York to make a real go of my career. My mom was clear, though, that the family was not about to pick up their entire lives to follow my dream. So she started to give me the tools to live and travel on my own.

Every now and then, she stepped back and let me take charge, like the time we were traveling to Germany for a job and, because our first flight was delayed, I was in jeopardy of missing our connection—and the shoot.

"Ash, we're at this airport," she said. "We're going to Frankfurt. How should we get there?"

She knew we might have come all this way for nothing, and that I might not be able to get us to where we needed to be on time. But she didn't jump in; she let me handle the situation without a single word of advice. Sure enough, I realized that if we waited for the next connecting flight via our original route, we wouldn't make it on time. But if we connected through an entirely different European country with a different airline, we would land with time to spare. Thanks to me and me alone, we made the shoot (although our luggage did not).

Learning to travel on my own was the least of my mother's prerequisites for my becoming a model. She also insisted that I finish high school before I made the move to the Big Apple. It was clear to everyone—including my teachers—that I was no student. I found school incredibly boring as well as hard. And the more classes I missed for modeling, the harder it got. Still, my mom felt it was important for me to have all the experiences that went along with high school, including prom.

(Now, prom has to be one of the most overrated experiences of all time, which I told my mom after I went. "Well," she said, "now you know: prom's overrated.")

The other formative American teenage rite of passage both Mom and Dad insisted I experience was the part-time job. In my case, it was working at Braeda, a café-style restaurant chain in Nebraska. Although I was already making nearly six figures annually as a model, my parents said I had to stick out the minimum-wage job for an entire year. Mom explicitly said that although I was already making "more than some doctors," she wanted me to know also what it was like to make minimum wage. My family placed value in understanding how other people lived, whether it be by washing dishes or walking runways.

It worked. I gained a sense of the responsibility necessary even in handling fast food, and nobody at that job gave me any kind of special treatment. My coworkers knew I was a model, because they might have seen me in a Kmart ad or on boxes of bras in Walmart. They were nice about it but not all that impressed.

"Oh, that's so fun!" people would say to me. To them, modeling seemed more like a hobby than a career. None of them really believed that I'd do it as my full-time job one day. But then, they didn't know me very well.

When graduation time finally came, I was more than ready to pack my bags and wave good-bye to Nebraska, Braeda, Mom and Dad, Kmart ads, and all the rest. I was seventeen, I had been traveling the world and making good money. It was go time!

Not so fast. Mom had one more stipulation.

By this point I knew many young models who had already moved to New York to make a go of their careers. Many of them, however, also had part-time jobs, such as bartending or waitressing, to make ends meet. Again, my mom brought her particular brand of Midwestern farm-town wisdom to the table.

"You can try living in New York for a year," she said. "In that year, I don't want you taking any jobs other than modeling. Your dad and I will help you out if you need money, but if after a year, you can't make it on your own, only modeling, you are coming back and going to college."

And that was that.

At my graduation party, I knew this was the last time I would be living in my mom and dad's house. No matter what rules my mom set out for me, I was sure it was all going to work out. But then again, I didn't have anyone to tell me what I now tell any girl who wants to be a model— that nothing, not even modeling, can ensure you'll be rich or famous—or feel pretty.

Ashleygram

How to photograph like a model. I can't promise you instant fame and fortune, but I can help you feel your best about snapshots and selfies. Here are some tricks that always work for me.

Start with some positive self-talk. Before you pose for a photo, take a second to remind yourself that you are beautiful, your body is beautiful, and that confidence makes everyone glow.

Know your best angles. Everyone's are different. Full-length mirrors are your friend.

Practice natural facial expressions while doing your makeup.

Always push your shoulders down. Most women hold their stress in their shoulders, and keeping them high can make your neck look short in a photo.

Know your go-to smile for a quick candid pic (from your friend, the full-length mirror).

If you want to create a waist, put your hands around the smallest part of your torso and then move your fingers slightly toward the center of your belly to create an hourglass effect. If you're shaped like a V, wider at the top and thinner legs, then fake a waist. Put your hands somewhere on your torso that feels natural and comfortable and then move your hand toward your navel slightly, but not all the way, to create the illusion of a waist. Try it in front of a mirror until you get comfortable with what looks and feels natural.

chapter 2

My Vagina:
With Great Power Comes Great Responsibility

Don't fall into the trap of sacrificing your self-esteem for affection and acceptance. No matter what your size, you are a sexy goddess. Remember that.

In a red bikini top and cutoffs, my legs up on the bar, I was holding court at the Mexican resort's restaurant. Sipping my nonalcoholic drink, surrounded by middle-aged men, I was having a grand old time—that is, until my mom found me.

"What are you doing?" she yelled, ripping me from my bar stool.

"Hey!" one of the men protested.

Wrong move.

"Do you realize she's *twelve years old*?" my mother screamed.

My poor mom. I wish I could say this scene during a family vacation to Mexico was out of the ordinary, but the truth is that this kind of attention from men arrived pretty early in my life.

I got boobs while we were living in Arkansas. I was still in fourth grade when my mom showed up one day to have lunch with me and a conversation—about my getting a bra and wearing it every day as part of my uniform. So, by the time I was eleven and in middle school, I had a woman's body.

My first experience of its power came when family friends were staying with us in Texas and their eighteen-year-old son surprised me in the laundry room, where we used to change and dry off after using the swimming pool. He had a huge erection that he showed me. Dripping wet from swimming, I just stood there until he took my hand and put it on his penis. "That's what you did to me," he said. I was ten years old.

I was scared and quickly ran away, but the moment left

me with so many lingering questions. What did he see that made his body change like that? Did I do something to make that happen?

My initial fear gave way to curiosity, which eventually turned into what I then believed was self-confidence. By the time we moved to Nebraska, when I had just turned twelve, I loved to flirt and be flirted with. At the first modeling convention I attended, when I was twelve (the one where I was signed by Wilhelmina), I spent most of my time with two boys who were also trying to become models. Paul and Scott, both at least five years older than me if not more, were always trying to get me alone. "Come into the hot tub with us," Scott said one night. I really wanted to, but I knew that my mom and dad would kill me if I did. So I said, "I'll be there," but never showed up. When I wore braided pigtails for one of the events, Paul came up behind me and said, "Ooh, blow job with handles." I didn't know what a blow job was, but I started laughing to make it seem as if I did.

It didn't matter how inappropriate, unsolicited, or confusing it was—any male attention was good attention as far as I was concerned. When I was on a plane at fourteen years old, and a man my father's age handed me an origami heart made out of a twenty-dollar bill, I didn't find it creepy in the slightest. And even though I knew I'd never call the number in the letter that I found inside the heart, I was still flattered.

My mom, who was usually traveling with me, wasn't. In the hope of protecting me, she was always trying to put a stop to leering men. Recognizing that I liked it when guys noticed me, she put all her effort into repelling them when they did. In Mexico, on the same trip where she ripped me away from the bar, she paid my little sisters (who are four and five years younger than me but at the time looked *much* younger) to run up to me and shout, "Mom! Mom!"

She didn't just try to embarrass me out of these dangerous flirtations; she also tried talking to me about why they were dangerous. "That is not where your self-worth comes from," Mom said. "These men can't give you that. You have to learn that yourself."

That's not the way it felt, though. I liked male attention. No, strike that. I loved it. I craved it, even. I know now that this is because I never got the love and attention I needed from my dad.

If you had asked me when I was a kid if I wanted my dad to pay attention to me, I would have screamed, "No way!" The house was a lot more comfortable when he wasn't around—which was most of the time, as I've mentioned.

Despite it all, when he took each of us out for our birthdays once a year, it was a huge deal and something we really looked forward to. I'll never forget my last birthday date with Dad, when I turned ten.

"You have to dress up," my mom said. "Daddy's taking you somewhere really fancy."

She didn't have to say it twice. This was back when rug shirts were in style, so naturally I had one. I paired it with black pants and curled my bangs. I felt so cool.

On our birthday dates, my dad was a totally different person. He held my hand when we arrived at our destination, The Ball! The huge skyscraper, officially Reunion Tower, got its nickname for the big ball on top that turns to give visitors a 360-degree view of Dallas—and that's where my dad and I were headed now. As we went up fifty stories in a huge elevator and then into the all-glass restaurant with the skyline twinkling outside, I couldn't have felt more glamorous.

If fathers are the model of male behavior for their daughters, then the one my dad presented me was contradictory. There was the magic of birthday dates, when we had his undivided attention and he made such an effort to make things special. And then there was everyday life, when he could be quick to get angry and aggressive. In a way, my father's one piece of advice to me regarding men sums him up perfectly: "Don't let him have sex with you, and make sure he opens the door for you."

Armed with that wealth of information, I started my dating life at sixteen. The only reason I waited that long is because that was the rule my parents laid down. There were certainly boys who showed interest long before I was sixteen. My first boyfriend, Craig, showed up at my house to pick me up for our date wearing a suit and tie!

"What in the world?" my mom said. "Why is he doing that?"

"That's strange," my dad said.

My dad could say whatever he wanted. I liked Craig. A lot. He was a bad boy. A skater and an artist, he smoked Vanilla Black and Mild cigars, which tasted good when we made out.

But we dated for only about three months of my junior year before he broke up with me. After picking me up at my house, he told my mom we were going to go for a walk in the park. Immediately I could tell something was up.

"What's going on?" I asked.

"I have to break up with you," he said, "because you won't have sex with me. And I'm afraid you're going to be as fat as my mom."

He flat out said this to me and nearly knocked me to the ground with his words. I couldn't believe it. Not that he would be so bluntly cruel (and, looking back, stupid) but that he was actually *breaking up* with me.

I had just had a phone conversation with his mom about what a good influence I was on Craig.

"He really likes you," she said. "He's never done his homework before, and he's doing it now because you're making him more responsible."

With the words that have been uttered so many times by so many women, I pleaded with him, "But we're so good together . . . and you are doing your homework now."

Craig was not persuaded, and that was the end of our love affair.

I had never felt uglier, fatter, and more disgusting in my whole life. All of a sudden I made the correlation between sex, my weight, and men. Craig's mom was obese. How could anyone, let alone someone who had touched my body, make a connection between the two of us? Everything I'd heard was now mixed up into one big cloud of insecurity. My dad telling me to lose weight for modeling and not to have sex . . . Craig breaking up with me because I was fat and wouldn't have sex with him. In that moment my daddy issues crystalized into how I related to men and saw myself in their eyes.

Thus started a pattern of going out with anyone who thought I was hot or my body was attractive. I lost my virginity to the school quarterback simply because he gave me some attention. It wasn't long after Craig and I broke up. Pete and I had computer class together even though he was a senior, and he started to give me little compliments about my appearance. "Ashley, you look really pretty today" or "I like it when you wear your hair like that."

A few of my girlfriends were hanging out with Pete's friends one night, so I decided to hang out, too. "You want to go downstairs?" he asked me.

"Sure."

We went downstairs and started to make out. He took my clothes off, and I took his off. I felt like we were filming a hot scene from a movie. Then, all of a sudden, he said, "I've got a condom."

In a split second, I decided.

"Okay."

What made my willingness to lose my virginity to a guy I didn't know even more incredible was that I was raised to believe that sex before marriage was a Sin. With a capital S.

My sisters and I were raised in the church. Church every Sunday. Church every Wednesday. I did all kinds of Christian summer camps. I know any and every Christian song that you can imagine. We had special vests, and for every new Bible verse memorized, we received a jewel to wear on them. My vest was always the most blinged out.

When we moved from Texas to Nebraska, I didn't like our new church, because it was very cliquey. I started to disconnect from my faith. Anytime I went to church it was more about clocking in for attendance, not developing a deep relationship with God. A big deal was always made about saving yourself until marriage, but the only reason to do that was because God wanted you to. And I guess that just wasn't a good enough reason for me.

Not only did I have sex before marriage, I did it with someone who I quickly realized didn't care about me at all. The next day at school when I went up to say hi to him in the hall, he ignored me. He never called me once. He didn't want anything to do with me.

Just like with Craig, I felt ugly and disgusting. But on top of that, I also felt used. In order to keep myself from drowning in self-loathing, I had to talk myself out of the deep regret I knew in my heart: "You screwed up by having sex before marriage, and now you want to have a pity party about this guy not talking to you?" I basically bullied myself into getting over it. Who cares? Just keep it moving. (I also went around telling anyone who would listen that he had a small penis. That helped me feel better, too.)

The worst part of this story, which has so many bad parts, is that a few months later, when I saw Pete at another party, we slept with each other again! I prized validation of my sex appeal through male attention so highly that I was willing to sacrifice my self-respect to get it. Ugh.

I think the next part of this tale is pretty obvious by now, right? I mean, if you suffer from the kind of daddy issues I had, moving to New York is just about the most dangerous place you can land. When I got out of Nebraska and my parents' house at seventeen to start my modeling career in Manhattan, I could do anything I wanted—and I did.

I wouldn't have said I was sleeping around like crazy. There was a rhythm to my interactions that went something like this: a guy would take me out; we would have sex the next time we saw each other; and then I wouldn't hear from him ever again. It was that quintessential sex-and-no-third-date situation.

Of course, I could have held out and refused to have sex before there was any sign of emotional attachment. But my euphoria also rested in sex. That was the moment, when I was the sole focus of a man's attention, when I was happiest. And if it meant I had to be slutty in the eyes of some, so what?

It also meant I never had a boyfriend. For the next two years after moving to New York, I lived a strange contradiction where I sacrificed long-term connection, i.e., a real relationship, for that immediate hit of adoration through sex. The result was a lot of loneliness, but as I had done when I lost my virginity to the quarterback, I continued to bully myself to get over it and keep on moving.

Then, when I was nineteen, I met Carlos. A muscular, Dominican web designer, he was a bad boy with a good job. Our chemistry was immediate from the moment we met outside a bar, but he told me that he didn't want to sleep with me until he knew that we were going to be together. Man, was that a turn-on!

Well, it didn't take long for him to become my first real boyfriend. It's funny, because I was a young, successful model in New York City, but Carlos won me over by making me feel beautiful. He thought my body was a temple. He touched me in a way that no man had ever touched me before. He wasn't afraid to be around me when I was naked. He *wanted* to see me naked. "You don't think that my cellulite is gross? Or that my breasts are saggy?" I asked. "What about my lower belly?"

"You're hot," he said.

"I am?"

He transferred the security he had with his physicality and sexuality to me, and it felt so good to feel finally good about myself.

I had never been in a real relationship before, so I didn't know how it was supposed to work. Ten years older than me, Carlos took charge of everything, and soon we were inseparable. He wanted us to be together every single day and definitely every night. I had a lot of fun in the beginning. We had lots and lots of sex. I really enjoyed being around him, and I loved being wanted.

As with all relationships, though, when the initial fog of attraction lifted, I started to actually get to know him. The picture of Carlos that came into focus was that of a sad, lonely man. Having been abandoned by his mother at a very young age, he found other ways to cope. He drank heavily every single night. The more comfortable he got with me, the more he drank.

One night about a year after we started dating, he was drunk, as usual, and I pissed him off by questioning him. I can't remember what it was about—maybe his finances or a friend, the typical stuff couples argue about—but he got so angry, he flipped the couch I was sitting on upside-down. I tried catching myself, but all my body weight landed on my right elbow. I'm surprised it didn't break. I probably should have gone to the hospital. But I didn't.

I definitely should have broken up with Carlos at that moment, but I didn't do that either. He had never been aggressive like that before, and I felt sorry for him. We were so far into it that I couldn't just walk away. I had to try to help him.

As his drinking got worse and worse, though, I stopped wanting to be around him. Eventually, I told him that I was thinking about our relationship and that maybe it was time to break up. The next night, when he let himself into my apartment, he was completely drunk. We started to fight, and he quickly picked up a butcher knife and chased me around my kitchen table. Terrified he was going to kill me, I locked myself in the bathroom.

Clearly I wasn't thinking straight, because I didn't call the police; I called my mother. Through sobs, I told her that Carlos was in a rage outside my bathroom door, and that I was afraid of him and what he might do to me. She asked me if I wanted her to talk to him, which I did, so I slipped my cell phone under the door and begged Carlos to talk to her. As he talked to her, he started crying, apologizing, and describing how messed up his life was. She continued to talk to him until he finally passed out on the couch.

The next morning I put my foot down. "We can't be together," I said. But he cried and cried, and I caved. And so began the next phase of our relationship, where he got drunk and violent, I threatened to leave, Carlos cried, and I stayed. There was always a reason. His father disappeared when he was a kid; his mother basically abandoned him too; his half brother and sister treated him as if he were totally unwanted. I worried he'd fall apart if I wasn't by his side. All of those things were true but not the real reason why I couldn't just walk away. I was addicted to the desire of a man who needed fixing. He said he couldn't survive without me, and I needed to be wanted.

I was so ashamed of the dynamic that I hid our relationship from all my friends and family. They'd ask me to meet them, or try to make plans, and I'd flat-out lie that I was flying out for a job and couldn't. I was so ashamed to be putting up with Carlos's behavior that I refused to go out in public with him and see him only at home, where nobody could run into us. Yet I didn't have the will to leave him.

I kept that juggling act up for an entire year until, one night while I was at his place in Queens, he got so angry at seeing some guy's profile pop up on my Facebook page that he threw a glass bottle at the wall, which shattered all over me. "That's it," I said. Of course, I had said that about a million times before, but this time I meant it. After a year of dating and nearly another year of hiding our relationship, my anxiety was at an all-time high. I didn't want to live like a recluse anymore. I knew I could do better and that I deserved more out of a relationship. What really woke me up wasn't the shattered glass but a fight I'd had earlier with my best friend, Rachel, who was so upset when I divulged to her that I had been seeing Carlos.

"You are worth more than this guy is able to give you. I foresee this turning into something terrible for your future," she said. "If you can't see it, you aren't the Ashley I thought you were." In that moment, Rachel made me see myself from the outside and reminded me of my power. (That's what best friends are for.)

No one could stop the cycle but me, but it was a struggle. Just because I'm pretty doesn't mean that I wasn't insecure. I slept around and stayed in an abusive relationship for affection and validation, because I thought I was too fat to find anything better. Finding power in your vagina is about realizing that you will never find acceptance and validation through a man. As hard as it is, owning who you are and knowing what you want is the only sure path to affirmation. It doesn't matter what you look like, how smart you are, or what kind of job you have; it's easy to lose control of the situation and find yourself in a violent or degrading relationship. But I want women to know they can get out of any situation if they return to their core source of strength: themselves.

The negativity from my destructive relationship with Carlos continued to reverberate after it ended. I knew I'd played a huge part in our dynamic, but I couldn't figure out what exactly my issue was. I was so scared of winding up with a guy like Carlos again that I knew I had to reflect on what attracted me to and kept me with him. I needed to figure how I had arrived at this place and reevaluate what I wanted out of men. There were only two things I knew for sure: in order to truly understand these things, I had to be single for a time and get my relationship with God straightened out.

In our family, the church is always there for you. If you were going through something bad and needed to get yourself out, the church was always the way to do it. Because my mom used the church as a support system when we were growing up and moving around constantly, she insisted I find a church when I first moved to New York.

Or, rather, she found it for me—a satellite congregation of the church we had attended while living in Dallas. And she went with me when I visited it for the first time. At that point I was not interested. I assumed that the people in the church in New York would not be people I could relate to. "Mom, I'm not about these people," I said, thinking I was cooler than all of them. "They don't get fashion, Mom."

My mom, used to my drama, wasn't having any of my attitude.

"You have to go six times," she said. "You can't know if you don't like something if you haven't tried it at least six times."

And so I began a tenuous relationship with church as an adult, attending now and then over the next three years.

But once I decided to refocus on myself and my work, it was the first place I went. I didn't go there to find a boyfriend; I wasn't looking for anyone other than the person I wanted to be, and to do that I knew I had to establish a real relationship with the Lord. That was the only way I could understand my life and my purpose.

In addition to attending services, I volunteered every Sunday. Again, it was my mom who drilled it into me that you don't just *go* to church; you also have to be of service. "Serving the church is like serving the Lord," she said. "It's also a humbling experience for someone with a life like yours." A few years earlier I would have just rolled my eyes at her, because I was loving everything about that life. But now, I needed more. I actually liked helping out and being with my community. Turns out, a lot of interesting people do.

My jobs were often to show people to their seat, give them a bulletin before they walked in, or open the door for them if they needed help. On one particular Sunday, seven months after breaking up with Carlos, my volunteer position was to take people up the elevator and direct them where to go.

That week, the church was holding a program called Porn Sunday where the pastor talked about the perils of pornography. I was thoroughly enjoying myself, standing in the elevator with a basket of candy, saying, "Welcome to Porn Sunday," and then pushing the button to the eighth floor. I always love shocking people if given the opportunity.

Two tall men about my age walked into the elevator, but I didn't bat an eye.

"Welcome to Porn Sunday!" I said. "That's right, we're going to talk about porn today."

I remember I was wearing my hair down that day, long and curly. I had thrown on a purple tank top and light-colored jeans with rips in them. I was so effortless that day; I couldn't have cared less what I looked like. I learned later that one of the guys nudged the other and said, "If you don't talk to her, I am."

All I knew in the moment was that his friend left the elevator, but he stayed on to ride back down with me.

I shrugged my shoulders. Even if I were looking for a man, and I wasn't, he definitely wasn't my type. With his short hair, ill-fitting, baggy Old Navy jeans, white Hanes T-shirt, and Converse sneakers, he exuded a major nerd fac-tor. There *was* something sweet about him, though. Plus, it was church. I was going to be polite.

"What's your name?" he asked.

"I'm Ashley," were the words I said, but my tone said, "Leave me alone."

He was undeterred: "I'm Justin."

After he rode the elevator up and down with me a few times, I got really annoyed.

"So what? Are you going to be like my security or some-thing?"

"Yeah, I'm your security. And you're my elevator lady."

When he sent me a Facebook message the next day, he did so as "Security," addressing me as "Dear Elevator Lady." After exchanging messages and seeing each other at church for a couple of weeks, Justin asked me out for coffee. I had learned through our messages a bit about him. He was different than most guys I'd met—and not just because he was nerdy. He was smarter and had traveled the world. He'd lived in Florence, Italy, for a while and spoke Italian. I was a little intimidated but agreed to the date.

To meet him that day, I wore black jeans and a purple, Moroccan-style flowing silk shirt with a gold band around the bottom, so that it still showed my figure (but not too much). I left my hair down and curly, the way I'd worn it that day in the elevator. We had a really great time. He seemed to be looking into my soul when he talked to me, but he was also funny. I was happy I had agreed to the date.

When the check for our two coffees arrived, I went to the bathroom. I had just assumed he'd take care of the bill, but when I returned, the check was resting on the table with his half on top. "Here you go," he said, handing me the bill.

"Oh, okay. I get it. You're not going to pay for my half."

I paid my half of the $5.25 and thought to myself, He has no money, or he's cheap. Either way, this is the last date.

When I told my mom and friends about what happened, they agreed. First date = last date.

The only person who didn't think splitting a five-dollar check on a first date is a deal-breaker was Justin. For a month, he called, texted, emailed—and I ignored it all. Finally I ran into him at church, which I had been avoiding in order to avoid him. Justin wanted to know what was going on and why I hadn't responded to him. If I had to explain it to him, he definitely wasn't the right guy for me. I tried to brush him off: "I just don't think this is really going to work out. . . ."

"Let me take you out for coffee. And this time, I'll pay," he said. "You like your coffee black, right?"

So I agreed to go out with him again. It wasn't just his persistence. When I saw him at church that day, it was one of those moments. He had a charm and charisma about him that made me almost forget what had happened. If a guy can make you forget something as annoying as not paying for your coffee, there has to be something there. Right? My mom thought I was nuts. "You need to go to counseling. You have issues," she said. But I liked Justin and wanted to give him at least one more try.

When it came time to pay for our falafels, I gave him a blank stare. He knew exactly what was going on.

"Let me explain," he said. "I'm going to pay for our dinner tonight. And I'm going to pay for our dinner tomorrow night, and I'm going to pay for the dinner after that. . . . When you told me you were a model, I assumed you were one of those beautiful women who uses guys for a fancy dinner. I don't play that game. I make my own money. I do well for myself, and I've also been burned because of it. I don't want to go out with anyone who only has me around so I can pay for stuff."

And, like that, I had my first experience of what it meant to communicate with a man. It was so new and profound that all I wanted to do after that was keep talking to Justin. We spent every single day together having great conversations. He is so smart. The consistency and openness I discovered while around him was so new to me that it just felt weird. And I told him this all the time: "You're weird."

From that moment on, we broke any and every rule of dating you can imagine—except for having sex. For Justin, abstinence was a firm commitment to his faith. For me, it had as much to do with my relationship to myself as it did my relationship with God.

Our early romance was innocent and sweet. Justin cooked for me. We would go rollerblading and biking. We went to the movies and even took an improv class together. Because we weren't sleeping together and never tempted ourselves by going over to each other's apartments late at night, we would have "twenty-four-hour dates." (That's what we called them, but in reality they were about twelve hours, ending at 6 a.m.) Basically, we'd hang out through the night, all over New York City. We went to late-night movies or took walks through parks. There was always a restaurant open somewhere, because it's New York City. We had a spot on Fourteenth Street and Seventh Avenue where we loved to sit and chat. We did karaoke with all of Justin's friends one night and while singing Beyoncé's "Single Ladies," I decided to drop low and my pants split all the way up the back. Another night, we walked the West Side and sat on the rocks by the piers. It was so romantic.

Despite how wonderful everything was with Justin, I kept a part of myself in reserve. A big part of me. While he offered so much of himself through our conversations, I kept on answering his probing questions with this: "If I know you in six months, I'll tell you."

It was odd that I chose to shut off when a truly great guy was offering me more than I could have ever imagined. Maybe it was simply the aftereffects from my abusive relationship with Carlos, or the cumulative effects of all the bad experiences I'd had with men over the years, starting with my father. Or maybe I didn't know how to love the right guy. I'm not sure, but I decided I didn't want to be his girlfriend just yet. And until the point that I did, I wasn't going to kiss him on the mouth, either. I went from one extreme to the other.

Justin didn't pressure me, but after one of our twenty-four-hour dates, four months into knowing each other, he understandably launched into the what-are-we-doing-here conversation.

"I really like you, and I really want to be your boyfriend," he said. "Will you be my girlfriend?"

And so, I said yes. Four months seemed like enough time to make the decision. But I regretted it right away. Part of me was afraid the label might ruin everything, like it had with Carlos. Mainly, though, it was because our first kiss was terrible. To this day, Justin says I'm the worst kisser he ever met, and that he had to teach me how to kiss. But I say the exact same thing. He claims I was giving him way too much tongue action. To me, he was a wet blanket.

Either way, the result of our bad make-out session was that we were officially boyfriend-girlfriend. But I felt like it wasn't right, and two days later I told him just that: "I don't think I can do this. I like who we are. I like what we're doing. I just don't want to be your girlfriend." Justin was understandably upset. Still, he told me to take my time.

But when Justin overheard me telling a girl in our improv class (who thought he was hot) that he was my boyfriend, he ran out of patience. In a cab home from class, he drew a line in the sand. "You called me your boyfriend. I'm not your boyfriend," he said. "You can't flip a switch and have me when it's convenient for you. I'm not going to wait for you forever."

I gasped because I felt like I had been physically punched. It hit me, not just from his words but also his truly hurt and honest tone, that *I* was playing a game. I thought of Justin as a boyfriend and treated him like one. Why wouldn't I want him to be my boyfriend?

I took a couple of weeks to do some serious soul searching, looking back on my relationship history with men, and recasting myself not as a victim but as a woman worthy of what she really wanted. Using my bad first kiss with Justin as an excuse for why we shouldn't be together was as much a red herring as thinking "good sex" was the reason I kept going back to Carlos. It can be easier to focus on the physical, especially when the emotional takes so much more work. The chemistry between Justin and me was undeniable, and because of the depth of the emotional connection we had made, I expected our first kiss to be magic. But, in our relationship, the physical followed the spiritual, which was the exact opposite of how I had always operated in the past. That's what I wanted. Justin was who I wanted.

If I had any lingering doubts that Justin was a good man, they were completely expelled when he came home with me to Nebraska. Things had moved pretty quickly between us after we made our relationship official. Within a few months, we had exchanged I-love-yous, and Justin had expressly said, "I see you as my wife."

Now, I should probably mention here that Justin is black. Before moving to New York City, I was ignorant about most of African American culture. I didn't grow up around many black people, and the sum total of what I learned in school was Martin Luther King Jr., Rosa Parks, and the Underground Railroad. That was nothing compared to my mom, who, raised in Nebraska, didn't even see a black person in real life until she was eighteen years old.

I never told Justin any of this, and I never told my grandparents that the man I was bringing home was black. I don't know what I was thinking. I guess I naively hoped everyone would be more open minded. That's not what happened.

When my grandparents met Justin, my grandmother was cordial but cold. She greeted him and then immediately walked away. When it came time for them to go, they didn't even acknowledge him. Instead, my grandmother looked me in the eye, with Justin standing right behind me, and said, "Tell that guy I said good-bye."

I had never seen my loving, hardworking, and wonderful grandma be so inconsiderate, hurtful, and racist. I was in shock.

After they left, I took Justin on a ride to get out of the house.

"Racism is never surprising," he said, "but always disappointing."

He explained that I would never understand the social burden of what it means to be a black person in America, but, he said, "If you're going to be my wife, this always has to be a conversation and a priority for you." From then on out, we never stopped talking about any and all issues, including white privilege, passive racism he encounters walking down the street, and overt racism that gives rise to movements like Black Lives Matter.

Justin made me understand that someone like my grandma only saw black men depicted on television in situations involving guns, rape, and violence—situations that perpetuate racist stereotypes against black people in general and black men in particular. She probably had never looked a black man in the face, let alone had a conversation with him, and now one was in her daughter's home, dating her granddaughter. (Similarly, he has helped me to see the ignorance that I perpetuate in my thinking at times. Just because I'm in an interracial relationship doesn't mean that I have black people "figured out" or that we live in a "postracial" society. Far from it, sadly.)

As if his understanding weren't generous enough, Justin took it upon himself to call my grandmother on her sixtieth wedding anniversary, because somehow he had remembered the date and that's what he does. He is not a texter. He's not an emailer. He's a pick-up-the-phone-and-call-you person. And anniversaries are a big deal to him. Grandma called my mom right after she got off with Justin, and said, "You'll never guess who called me." And from then on out, she loved him. *Loved* him.

I'm so grateful that happened, and it never would have if Justin hadn't put his hand out there. He always puts love above pride, which is what he did with me. When I was playing games, he called me out on it. When we began dating, he did it with intention, always asking the difficult questions, such as "What do you bring to this relationship?" and "What role do you see yourself in beyond a girlfriend or a wife?" I wasn't always sure how to answer. I didn't like my mom and dad's marriage, but I couldn't put my finger on why. Maybe it was that I didn't like my dad. But through constant communication with Justin, I envisioned a marriage that was more than just two people loving each other. It was also a partnership dedicated to building something bigger than ourselves.

It seemed fast to a lot of people when we got married. I was just twenty-two years old, and we had basically known each other only a year and a half. We didn't get married to have sex or to have the safety of the label "married." For us, marriage is about building a foundation that's so strong it not only helps us be who we want to be as individuals but also changes the lives of the people around us. With that in our hearts and heads, we tied the knot on August 14, 2010.

I'd be lying, though, if I said we weren't excited to have sex as well. We were so excited to be together, we didn't say good-bye to a single one of the ninety friends and family members at the restaurant where we got married. We grabbed our gifts and got out of there as fast as we could.

Back at home, the time had finally come. We were going to have sex!

I've talked a lot about my sexual relationships with other men, and I'm not going to go into detail about my sexual relationship with my husband. What I will say is that the sexual relationship that I have with Justin surpasses by leaps and bounds any and every relationship I've had in the past.

Just as important, though, is our verbal communication. Whether talking about race, how grateful we are that we found one another and waited to consummate our marriage, or ways in which we can excel in our professions, Justin and I started talking from the minute we met—and we haven't stopped since. That's something worth waiting for.

chapter 3

Put the Snickers Down

Every day is a new day and a new struggle. But with a little reflection, you can develop the tools to put that Snickers down or not care so much when you don't want to.

Size. Weight. The elephant in the room. I hate that I have to talk about it, but it's how I got to where I am. So here goes.

As for pretty much every thick woman I know, the comments on my body started early. I began developing breasts, hips, and everything else at ten years old. And I developed *fast,* so that by the time I was twelve, I looked like a woman.

If I'm being charitable, I'd say that the other kids were threatened. It must've been difficult to be faced with a girl in their class who looked like she could have been their baby-sitter. Their defensiveness from feeling this threat resulted in cruelty.

If I'm being honest, I'd say the other kids were a bunch of jerks.

The girls at school teased me mercilessly and made fun of me for my height, my build, and my big hair.

"Thunder Thighs."

"Cottage Cheese Thighs."

"Beep, beep, beep. Wide load coming through."

Name a fat joke or mean description for thighs, and I've heard it. The crazy thing was that I wasn't even fat. Not at all. I played sports and my body was perfectly proportional. I was just a big-boned, thick, strong girl. For the kids at my school who were morbidly obese, I can't imagine what the bullies called them. I didn't stick around long enough to find out. In middle school, it's every kid for herself.

When I was discovered by that modeling agency in a Nebraska mall, it was an enormous self-esteem booster. Most young women are looking for external validation of their beauty, but perhaps none more so than the curvy ones.

When I was signed to a major modeling agency, all the taunts from my classmates stopped cold. I was awash in the golden feeling of being told I was pretty.

I knew that I was a larger model but didn't understand what that really meant. The Midwestern modeling convention where the New York agents decided to sign me was where I first learned my category: plus-size. I didn't feel bad about that label, though, because Paul and Scott, the two boys I had crushes on at the modeling expo, told me, "We'd rather be with a girl that looks like you than some, like, twig."

I lapped it up, until those guys went off with the twigs.

Becoming a professional model was a double-edged sword when it came to my self-image. On one side I was given the validation that an industry had deemed me pretty. On the other side, I was setting myself up for public scrutiny—particularly when it came to my body. My very first editorial job for *YM* was textbook: the magazine spread featured three different body shapes: Apple for someone with a round stomach; Pear for big hips; and Cantaloupes for large breasts. I was Cantaloupes.

The kids in my eighth-grade class back home called me Cantaloupes for the rest of the year. (At some point, they shortened the nickname to Lopes.)

That, however, wasn't what bothered me most. When someone brought in the magazine to school, a girl pointed at my knees in the photo—more specifically at the creases where they bend.

"What's that on your knees?" she asked. *My flesh. That's what it is.*

That girl pointing out the folds on my knees made me feel really, really fat. It didn't matter that I was in a magazine that was being sold all over the country, something that would never happen for her. No, I just focused on my fleshy knees. I tortured my mom over my knees, and then I moved on to other parts of my body. As soon as I went through puberty, I got what my husband calls side-butt. I don't know what the name for it is; extra hip fat? When I discovered I had it, I yelled for my mother.

"Mom, look at this! What is this?"

"It's your hip, Ashley," she said.

"It's weird! It's disgusting."

"It's your hip! God gave it to you! Who cares?"

I cared—that's who.

No matter how many jobs I landed, I always found something to criticize about my appearance. And if I couldn't find a flaw, there were girls at school to help me out, no problem. During my senior year, when I was already doing quite well, one cheerleader (aka a very popular person) said to me, "You're not a model; you're just a fat model."

Devastated by the way this cheerleader had cut me down, I came home crying and told my mom what had happened.

"How much money do you think this cheerleader made this year?" my feisty mom said. "That big booty you have is making you big bucks. You got junk in that trunk that's making you cash. You go with it."

While my mom's use of slang made me cringe, I appreciated the pep talk. Mom told me something else that I knew I needed to learn. "No matter where you are, there will always be people like that."

What she meant by "people like that" was people who don't like you; people who want to tear you down, because they are jealous or angry. Mom told my sisters and me that no matter what kind of profession we entered, we would encounter people we didn't like—and that we would need to learn to work with them if we wanted to be successful. It was just like in school with certain kids or even some teachers. You can't quit algebra just because you don't like the teacher.

My mom's guidance helped me so much when I became a model. Whenever I encountered a difficult personality—whether it was a rude photographer or dismissive agent—my mom wouldn't let me go on and on complaining about how terrible so-and-so was. Instead she told me I had to change my mindset and "make it my job" to get whoever was troubling me to appreciate me for who I was. "If you can do that," she said, "think how easy it's going to be to work with everybody else."

When it came to self-acceptance, maybe this was the most important thing my mom imparted to me: that my size was heritage and something to be proud of. My mother is a big woman but always a specimen of health. She loves being tall and the way clothes fit her because of this. I always knew she was strong. On my mom's side, we are all just big. "Ashley, at age twelve you were a size twelve. You're fourteen now, and you're a size fourteen. At sixteen, you're going to be a size sixteen," she said during a visit to the pediatrician where I got upset about my weight. "You're a part of this big-boned family. This is the way we look and so it's the way you look. If you were a petite little thing, you would look funny. You wouldn't fit in."

Knowing where you belong—*that* you belong—is the greatest confidence booster anyone can have. (When it comes to my family, it helps that the group I belonged to is one I'm proud of as well.)

My mom might have done a little *too* good a job of making me feel good about myself no matter how much I weighed, because I continued to gain weight—a lot—even after I stopped growing. Once I moved to New York, I went from size 14 to 18 in about a year. And I was in New York to be a *model*.

In truth, my rapidly increasing dress size had less to do with my mom's words of wisdom and more to do with my love of chili cheese fries. Out on my own for the first time in my life, in a city where you can get whatever you want to eat whenever you want it, I ate . . . whatever I wanted. Usually chili cheese fries. I still love them, but at the time I probably had them every day. On top of that, I wasn't so keen on the exercise thing either. At most I hit the gym a couple times a week to walk on the treadmill or maybe lift a few light weights.

Like so many women exiting their teens, I didn't know how to manage my weight in a healthy way. It seemed like there were only two options: eat whatever I want or eat nothing.

I know which option my agents at the time wanted me to choose. They were always telling me I needed to lose weight. I dreaded those days when I had to go in and get measured more than anything else I've experienced in my life. More than finals. More than a root canal. Getting measured—which models do in order to make sure they can fit into sample sizes—was the scariest thing, ever. I would wear four pairs of Spanx and the thinnest pair of pants ever created in the history of pants in the hope of faking my measurements by a millimeter. Somehow, though, my agent always knew what was going on and made me strip down. It was like he had a special Spanx sense.

Part of the reason I dreaded getting my measurements taken was that there was such a wide range: when that tape measure came out, I never knew what the number was going to be—and sometimes I was in for a real shock. My hips could fall between 45 and 49 inches, my waist between 29 and 34. (My hips now go between 46 and 48 inches, my waist between 29 and 32. The only consistent numbers are my breasts, always the same 36DDD. The range of my measurements has shrunk because I have learned how to eat and exercise better. There are still fluctuations, though, depending on my schedule; if I'm on the road a lot for shoots, I can't always hit the gym and eat as cleanly as I should.)

Of course, it wasn't the number that was upsetting. If you're healthy, what does it matter if your hips are 45 or 49 inches? As my grandma said, "What's the problem? Just go up a size in your dress." Numbers are abstract. It's the human reactions to them that cause the hurt. In my case, what I couldn't stand were the conversations with my agents *after* I got my measurements.

I'll never forget one time when my numbers on the tape were on the higher side. An agent started fanning himself with a wad of money like some saloon prostitute in an old-fashioned Western.

"Hey, Ash, come here," he said. After I walked over to him, he fanned me with the bills. "If you want some more of this," he said, "you gotta drop the LBs, baby."

Another senior agent's favorite line was: "It's time for you to put the Snickers down."

Never mind that I didn't eat Snickers. I got the point.

"Just look as thin as possible going into this casting," I was told over and over, "because they like smaller girls."

This isn't just a message given to plus-size models like myself; it's one every woman is hit over the head with *all the time*.

Okay, but I am a model, and my weight is part of how I made a living, so it is fair game for scrutiny, right? I told myself that the fat comments were in my professional best interest. A lot of plus-size modeling is catalog work, and if you don't fit into the sample sizes, you won't land the job. No matter how much my measurements fluctuated, however, I always fit into the samples, because I was always proportionate in the breasts, hips, and waist. I was also never round in the middle (I always gain weight all over my body).

I had to admit, though, that the issue of my weight wasn't always treated with professionalism within the industry. Scratch that. It was hardly ever dealt with respectfully. How many times did I hear stylists snicker (there we go with snickers again) behind a plus-size model's back? Things like

"Can you believe that she's wearing a crop top?" Listening to some agents refer to models—*successful* models—as heifers or cows, I felt so insecure.

I received my own share of insults. One time while on a job in Germany, the stylist had to slice the jeans I was wearing up the back because they were too small, but we had to shoot them. She took a pair of razor-sharp scissors, and starting from the bend of my knee, glided them up my thighs until she got to my butt cheeks. When the jeans still didn't fit, the stylist then had to cut through the butt pockets. She said something in German and everybody laughed. I didn't need to understand the language to know she had said something about me. Later, when I asked someone to translate, I found out she had said, "If this big girl falls on me, we are both going to die. Her from the scissors and me, from her." I felt like the fattest person alive.

Now, looking back, I feel mad. This was their job as much as it was ours. You would think that the people whose career it was to represent curvy models in this industry would want to build us up, not tear us down. But at the time, the overheard snide comments or cruel names only reinforced my belief that I needed to lose weight. All I wanted to do was to conform to what people wanted from me.

There was just one problem. For me, losing weight was, and still is, an uphill battle. I'm the type who, if you tell me to lose weight, I gain it. If I put pressure on myself to lose it, I gain it. If I *think* about food, I gain it. My best friend loses weight when she gets depressed. Me? I gain it, and then it takes me ages to get the weight off. There are some people who can drop a few pounds for a job, wedding, whatever. I just can't. That's not how my body works. My weight was always a conversation. *Always.*

As the years went by, I started to notice a funny thing. No matter how much I weighed, I never stopped working, ever. Sometimes my agents threatened that if I didn't lose weight, I would lose a client. (You know what happened then; that only made me gain more weight!) Well, guess what? It never happened. If anything, I only grew more successful.

I landed one of my biggest paychecks when I was close to my heaviest. The job was a national Lane Bryant lingerie commercial, I was a size 18, and they *loved* me.

Although I had already worked for the plus-size retailer, this was a whole other level, a huge deal. Flying out to LA for a commercial being shot by a big-time Hollywood director, I was so nervous but also excited. I had met Justin by this time and was jetting off to a major shoot. It was hard not to feel like I was reaching the top of my game. Everything personally and professionally was finally coming together—and better than I could have ever hoped. Still, a small voice continued to nag at me: *But what about your size?*

At the shoot, walking on set, I couldn't afford to feel insecure, so I turned to a go-to defense mechanism I've seen so many curvy ladies employ.

"Have you ever been with a big girl before?" I said to the director, adding a hearty laugh. You know, throw that reality right in their face before anyone has a chance to throw it in yours (or quietly snicker about it behind your back.) This was for Lane Bryant. Of course they had been with a big girl before. But it helped me feel confident on the inside, which immediately translated to my outside.

Another model was supposed to be the lead in the commercial, but the director pronounced her "not pretty enough." He said, "It has to be Ashley. I'm not going to shoot it unless it's her." The director pulled rank—for me! So they switched the whole commercial to make me be the lead. It wasn't just flattering; it changed the trajectory of my career. I forged a lasting and important relationship with Lane Bryant, and my day rate doubled.

When I first met Justin, he asked me what I did for a living—a question that used to annoy me so much.

Because I am so big, I would always get a chip on my shoulder when I had to explain that, yes, I'm a model. No, not a hand model or a hair model but a real, full-on model. I've heard everything from "You have a really pretty face, I just don't understand the rest," to "I didn't know there were those kinds." Or, "Do you model from the neck up?" and "That's nice that they're representing women of your stature."

Yeesh.

I would get so defensive in those moments—sometimes, frankly, I turned into a straight-up mean girl. That's what I was like when Justin asked me what I did for a living, giving it over-the-top, hair-flipping attitude, "I'm a model." Justin told me later, it seemed as if I were saying I was way too good for him. How could he have known about my hang-ups? Thankfully he didn't let a little attitude stand in the way of pursuing me.

What's funny about Justin when it comes to my size is

that now that we're married, he makes me feel small. In a good way. You know how every woman wants to roll up in her man's arms? (Not every woman, but a lot of us.) It's about feeling safe and comforted—feelings that aren't always easy for a big girl like me. But that's exactly how he makes me feel, not only physically. I know that if any problem arises, he will take care of it. Financial, emotional, whatever the circumstances, Justin would be that hustler for me. It is a multitude of things that make me feel protected, and the physical is definitely wrapped up in there somewhere. With Justin, I have a type of body dysmorphia where I think I'm smaller than I am. So I'll go and jump on him or curl up and sit in his lap, at which point he'll joke, "My size two baby."

The thing about a woman's size is that it changes, and I don't mean through diet or age or anything like that. Our shape depends on our perception of ourselves and, unfortunately, on that of a lot of others who feel entitled to "weigh in" with their opinions on other people's bodies. As someone who's put herself out there so much, even appearing semi-naked in a national commercial, I knew I was opening myself up to public scrutiny. What I didn't realize at the time, though, was how wildly those opinions would swing.

I've been told that I'm not big enough to be a voice for curvy women. I've also been told that because I make "fat look cool," I'm going "to kill somebody."

As a model who embraces social media, I know this is par for the course—but sometimes I get fed up. Ironically, one of the toughest moments for me was when I was ridiculed not for being fat but for being too thin. It came after I posted a picture of myself from the set of *America's Next Top Model*. Not only did I have the confidence of a new job as a judge on the awesome TV show started by one of my heroes, Tyra Banks, but I was also wearing a killer outfit: a white knit skirt, matching crop top, and Balmain leather jacket.

No sooner had I posted the picture than it went viral, but not for the reasons I had hoped. Instead of people being psyched at the image of a curvy woman looking superhot in high-end clothes usually only available in a size 2, they were pissed off.

"You don't make plus-size dollars anymore, you make backstabbing dollars."

"You don't love the skin you're in, you want to conform to Hollywood. You believe being skinnier is prettier."

"Fake fat person."

"Fame has made Ashley follow the herd, and lose her voluptuousness."

That's just a tiny taste of the angry comments that poured into my Instagram account. I was shocked and angry.

I was accused of transforming my body into a size 6 overnight, which was ludicrous. I shot back that if I could lose eighty pounds in a week, I wasn't a model but a wizard. I defended myself against public ridicule by arguing that my thin appearance in the pic was a testament to my abilities as a model. "I know my angles," I wrote.

But then I started to question why I had to defend myself in the first place. What gave people the right to comment on whether I gained or lost weight? It dawned on me that trying to please others was always going to be a losing proposition. Too fat, too thin, too loud, too quiet, I was never going to fit the standards others created for me. Instead of complying, I protested.

"I am more than my measurements," I wrote in an essay for Lena Dunham's online feminist newsletter *Lenny Letter*. "The cycle of body-shaming needs to end. I'm over it. . . . My body is MY body. I'll call the shots."

I decided to stand up for my beliefs when I thought about all the women in this world who get ridiculed for posting confident photos of themselves. When a woman feels beautiful and someone tears her down, it's not okay. I'm a model who uses social media to promote my message and brand. Criticism, fair or unfair, is going to happen. Still, I understand how much it hurts. The *ANTM* controversy might have made me mad. The social media uproar that erupted when *Sports Illustrated* posted its 2016 Rookie Reveal to Instagram, announcing I was going to be in the magazine's iconic Swimsuit issue, made me sad.

The comments were devastating. A bunch of men unloaded a series of insults.

"I can't believe you're putting this fat cow in this magazine. You're ruining it."

"What is this heifer doing in here? Her thighs are going to swallow the pages."

Some women were equally angry.

"I'm over here, working my ass off in the gym. But this fatty gets a spread in *Sports Illustrated*? What gives?"

This was the only time in my career that I cried because of things I read about myself. (Crying is an understatement; I was hysterical.) Like so many women, my first instinct was to internalize and validate these comments. *I'm ruining* Sports Illustrated. *I am fat . . . and terrible.*

Spiraling into the dark and negative is understandable, but it doesn't lead anywhere good. Luckily, I kept reading the comments on Instagram—and, as the day went on, both men and women came to my defense. Lots of them.

"I can't believe you would actually even say something so mean. Didn't your parents raise you better?"

"She's speaking out for so many different women that haven't been represented before. This is great."

"I prefer my women curvy. Finally, *Sports Illustrated* puts a woman I want to be with in their magazine."

Sports Illustrated doesn't do anything in one of its most lucrative issues of the year without market-testing the hell out of it. Before they admitted me to its pages, and certainly before putting me on the cover, someone from *SI* told me that I had to pass the approval of all different kinds of focus groups, from middle-aged women to thirteen-year-old boys. And guess what? *All* of them, including thirteen-year-old boys, wanted to see me in a swimsuit!

I truly believe that everything happens for a reason. I believe that you are better for the struggles you have endured. Difficult times will come your way, but it's how you handle them that makes you the person you are. Being the big girl, I've always had to work harder, be nicer, look more put together, anticipate needs quicker. Chances are you have, too. No matter what your job is, you've had to do things a little differently if you are a curvy woman. I have had to constantly justify my career choice over and over. But that might just be the secret to my success.

When you're not the norm, a lot more reflection is required of you. And while that might not be fair, introspection is never a bad thing. In so many ways, I know that being a different kind of model—a "new model"—and striving for success despite conventional wisdom is part of the reason why I am where I am. The other, even bigger, reason is that I've been cheered on by women just like me for putting myself out there. Everywhere I go, people tell me how I've inspired them by making curves look beautiful and speaking up for body diversity. All I know is that whatever I've put into defending myself and others like me is nothing when compared to what I have received in return.

chapter 4

When the Fun and Games Aren't Fun Anymore

How not to win friends and influence people—or feel good about yourself: over-the-top partying, shopping, paying for others, and sleeping around. Believe me, I tried all of that and more.

"Ashley, darlin,' salt or no salt on your margarita? I always forget."

That was Caitlin, my roommate when I moved to New York City at seventeen years old. Another plus-size model, she was porn-star hot with big fake breasts, bronzed skin from tanning beds, and long blonde hair. She was the quintessential California girl and a terrible influence.

The first time I met her outside our new apartment, a sublet on Twenty-fifth Street between Eighth and Ninth avenues, she was wearing her hair big and her tight dresses short. I didn't think I had ever met someone so sexy in my life.

I let Caitlin have the bigger bedroom because she was older. The apartment, a two-bedroom, one-bath, didn't come furnished, so we headed over to Rent-A-Center to get beds and furniture. The apartment itself was disgusting. When we opened up the kitchen cupboards, roaches came crawling out! We never cooked anything. I think maybe Caitlin cooked eggs, once.

But it didn't really matter that our kitchen was roach infested, because neither of us was in New York City to enjoy domestic life. We were trying to be models and have some fun in the process.

Because Caitlin was older, she already had a leg up on how and where to party, and she was more than game to show me the ropes.

This started with getting the right "going out" outfits. Caitlin knew all the stores—like Betsey Johnson and BCBG—where you could get the hip-hugging, thigh-high, cleavage-baring party dresses all the girls wore to the clubs.

We partied almost every single night; at least that's what it felt like. A lot of times I went out with Caitlin and my agents, who could get into all the hottest clubs in the city. Sometimes, though, it was just Caitlin and me, which presented more of a challenge. The first hurdle was that I was underage, and the bars and clubs had recently become really strict about checking IDs. Two underage girls had died of cocaine overdoses in a club that same year, so cops were everywhere.

"Ashley, you know what to do," Caitlin said when we approached the bouncers.

"Will you let us in if we flash our tits?" I asked. My mother would have been so proud.

Looking back, it was shameful, but, honestly, at the time, it just seemed like a smart and easy way to get into the club, because their answer was always yes.

Once inside, we didn't act much better, table-hopping to meet rich guys, mainly for the purpose of drinking their alcohol. Although we had money (probably not as much as those guys, but who knows), we acted like we didn't. Bottle service at Manhattan clubs can easily cost upward of four hundred dollars a person.

The whole scene was kind of a seedy game where we pretended to like these men—to what purpose? Just to drink their alcohol? We were working models and could have bought our own drinks, but what was the fun in that? It was a power play. Lording our youth and beauty over these men, we looked to see how much we could get away with. Sometimes, though, we took the game a little too far.

Once Caitlin and I ran up a huge tab at a young banker's table at a superexclusive club in the Meatpacking District. Between the two of us, we probably drank $500 in champagne. It was not cute. With every sip, we seemed to promise a little more until Caitlin and I found ourselves in a cab with him sitting between us, headed back to our apartment to "hang out." When we got to our place, he started to pay the driver. Caitlin and I looked at each other, and then in a flash we both bolted from the cab and straight into our apartment. He didn't give up easily, though, and came running after us. Thank God, we got inside the vestibule before he caught up. Still, he was banging on the front door, yelling, "You owe me all this money from tonight! You promised me that I was coming up!"

As the red-faced man bashed his hand into our front door, I got scared. My heart thumped so hard in my chest I thought it was going to fall right out. Caitlin always put me in these sorts of situations, ones that I really didn't like and truly wasn't comfortable with. But it wasn't Caitlin's fault. The real issue was, why did I go along with them in the first place?

I had led such a sheltered life back home—even by Nebraska standards. It felt like I was never allowed to party like the other kids in my high school. I had to be home by 11 p.m. I wasn't permitted to date until I was sixteen. Now I was all alone and free—in a city 1,500 miles from home, and it's all right there for you, anytime you want it.

In my first three months in New York, I really got into partying with Caitlin. We didn't just drink but also experimented with drugs. I tried cocaine and Ecstasy. One night, after we took Ecstasy, we started at the downtown Ritz-Carlton and walked more than four miles up the West Side Highway to the Fifties, all the while sucking on Push Pops, the candy that you push up with your finger. By the time we got to Midtown, we had licked away all the candy, but we were so high we didn't realize it and were licking our fingers coming up from the bottom of the Push Pop holder. "Wow," I said. "We're really messed up."

No kidding. I was seventeen years old in New York City, *this* was my life, and Caitlin was my guide. I was getting drunk. I was getting high. I was dining on chili cheese fries almost every night; this couldn't be headed anywhere good. This wasn't who I was. Not at all.

Caitlin wasn't the reason for my bad behavior. As if to bring that point home, my worst partying incident wasn't even with her. It was a night that I went out with a bunch of other models. To make a long story short, I had three Long Island ice teas in thirty minutes—thirty minutes! (In case you aren't aware of the alcoholic nature of a Long Island iced tea, it's a mix of tequila, vodka, light rum, triple sec, gin, and a splash of cola. Ugh, just thinking about it now makes me feel ill.)

It's no surprise that I don't remember what happened next, but apparently I got kicked out of the bar because I was so loud. Then once outside, I fell on the sidewalk, and nobody was strong enough to pick me up and get me in a cab.

Another model, the only sober one and the only one freaking out, called an ambulance.

As the EMTs loaded me into the ambulance, according to my friend, I said, "I'm eighteen. You can't call my mom and dad."

"What's their number?" one of them asked, and I blurted it out.

I don't remember any of this, but the ambulance took me to the hospital, where I eventually woke up in a row of homeless people and other patients, strapped down to my bed because apparently I had been kicking and fighting. They didn't pump my stomach, because I didn't technically have alcohol poisoning. I'd just had way too much to drink.

"We called your parents," said a clearly annoyed nurse. "You can go."

Truly upset now, I went straight to the apartment of one of the junior agents from my agency. Why did I decide to go to this guy's house? I don't know. It was the first place that came to mind. After I told him what had happened, he asked, "Are you okay?"

"Yeah, I'm fine," I lied.

"Well, you know we have to tell the boss tomorrow."

The agent who ran our division was kind of a father figure. If the news of my going to the hospital because I was so drunk got back to him—and I hadn't told him about it—that would be worse than if he heard it from me first.

Now I really felt sick. The junior agent said that if I didn't call him, I'd really be in trouble. The boss was older, and intimidating even when you hadn't done anything

76

wrong. He had the right to ax any model for any reason—it could be cattiness, gaining too much weight, or disorderly conduct. He was kind of like the Wizard of Oz, pulling a lot of levers from behind a curtain so that we never got to see or understand.

I couldn't believe I had to interrupt his weekend on a Sunday to tell him I had wound up in the hospital from binge drinking. As it turned out, I was interrupting his weekend at a baseball game.

"Hi, how are you?" I asked, cool and casual.

"I'm fine," he said. "Ashley, you're calling me on a Sunday. I'm at a baseball game. What's wrong?"

"I just have to tell you that I was in an ambulance yesterday, and it was because I drank too much."

"What did your mom and dad say?"

"I haven't called them yet. I'm too afraid."

"Look. You messed up, but the important thing is that you are alive and okay. But you have to tell them."

I was grateful that he took such a calm and protective approach to the news. I guess it wasn't such unusual behavior for a model to go out and go crazy.

As for my parents, they didn't need to be told—the hospital had already taken care of that for me. I needed to face the consequences. I knew that for my mom, one of the worst possible phone calls she could get would be a call from a New York City hospital saying that her underage daughter was there for an alcohol overdose. I dreaded placing that call, but I knew it had to happen.

"I don't know what to do here in Nebraska," said my

mom, who was just as devastated as I thought she'd be. "Dad and I think you need to go to rehab."

"Rehab!?"

She arrived in New York the next day. We had it out. She worried about my emotional and physical safety. I told her she was overreacting. This was the equivalent of my college experience. Yes, I was going to make mistakes, but who doesn't? The only difference between a college kid and me was that I was making my own money.

I'm not sure who won the argument. I didn't have to go to rehab, and my mom didn't try to get closer to me or monitor my life in any way. Instead she gave me my space. Well, sort of.

She didn't call me all the time (because she had that mom wisdom that when kids are doing something their parents wouldn't approve of—in my case, getting drunk and sleeping around—they push them away). Because I was doing things that my mother didn't like, we probably spoke only once every couple weeks. Instead of talking over the phone, she began reaching out by sending me little care packages. In them were my favorite desserts wrapped in tinfoil, books, household things like chip clips that were useful but only a mom would buy, pens, socks, little bottles of shampoo. But that's not all. She would always add a note with a verse from the Bible, like Philippians 4:6: "Do not be anxious about anything, but in every situation, by prayer and petition, with thanksgiving, present your requests to God." (This verse is on my vision board to this day.)

This approach might sound heavy-handed, but it was

actually the opposite. Mom wasn't preaching or even being the lecturing parent. The verses weren't her way of throwing my behavior in my face, calling me a sinner, or condemning me. They were little notes of love.

"I'm still here. I support you and I know you can do this," she wrote. "God's there to help you, and here's what he says."

My mother's way of getting closer to me while I was far away was the ultimate exercise in patience. She knew that although I opened those packages in my own time, I always got the message. I needed to learn on my own that the path I was taking, partying, drugs, being someone I didn't really know, wasn't the root to happiness, satisfaction, or confidence.

I was making up for never being the popular girl at home, so I wanted to be the popular girl in New York, no matter what it took. If I had to try any drug, laugh at every joke, drink more than anyone else, I was going to do it. So many curvy women do the same thing to themselves. We feel like we have to be the life of the party, or we don't deserve an invite. Because we don't feel like we can establish any boundaries, we end up on a very dangerous or demoralizing path.

The shape of your body doesn't have anything to do with how fun you are, and if anyone thinks otherwise, they aren't worth hanging out with. Well, I wish I had known that when I first moved to New York. It not only would have saved me a lot of bad experiences but a lot of money as well. My people pleasing also included picking up a lot of bar tabs.

Tied in with my bad behavior around alcohol and men were money troubles. When it came to finances, I had a lot of growing up to do. I was this amazingly lucky girl who was making $100,000 at seventeen, and blowing it within the year—without even knowing where the money was going.

Despite taking advantage of men in clubs, I paid for more than my fair share of bar tabs. I picked up the $2,500 bill for one of my best friend's birthdays. *Twenty-five hundred dollars!* And I paid for it because . . . I was the "catalog cash cow." It was almost expected that I would cover things for my friends, including by me. Maybe I felt a little guilty that I made more money than my peers, or I just wanted so much to be liked that I was happy to pay any price.

However, that's only one of the ways I threw away the money I was working so hard to earn. My other big expenditure was transportation. I did not know the subway system, so I spent all my money on cabs. It might sound like an exaggeration, but unless you've lived in New York City, you don't understand how much cash you can blow on taxis. Honestly, it's obscene.

It wasn't even an issue of luxury. My taxi habit was more about laziness than anything else. I didn't take the time to learn how to take the subway because, frankly, I didn't want to. I chalked it up to the fact that I drove everywhere growing up and wasn't going to stop now. If it was going to cost more money, it was going to cost more money. And besides, I was working hard. I had the money.

When tax time came after my first year in New York, I was hit with a real shock. That's when they realized I didn't have any money in my bank account to pay the hefty bill. I had no clue that the agency didn't take money out of my paychecks for taxes—and I had blown *everything*. My parents, who had helped me gather the paperwork together for my accountants to do my taxes, tried to do a forensic analysis of my year's spending habits, but it was futile.

"Where did this ten thousand dollars go?" asked my dad while looking over the statement provided by my agency that outlined what I had been paid that year.

"I have no idea," I said.

"What about this four thousand?"

"I don't know."

And I didn't. It seemed unfathomable, looking at those large numbers on the page, that I could have spent so much on eating out (breakfast, lunch, *and* dinner), rent, cabs, partying, and, oh yeah, shopping. A lot of my shopping came out of boredom. Growing up, going to the mall was a major pastime, even if I didn't have any money to buy anything. Young, lost in a big new city, and trying to make it in a very difficult career, I used retail therapy as a way to soothe myself and fill up any lonely hours.

Yup, my money was all gone. I had nothing, *nothing,* to show for my year of work.

When I moved out of the temporary sublet I shared with Caitlin, and into a high-rise apartment all of my own, I didn't know how to pay my own bills. My situation wasn't unique. So many young girls arrive in New York without a clue how to lead functioning adult lives—and there is no one to guide them. It's shocking and sad that there is no system or union to teach these new models how to manage their money and protect themselves. When I first arrived, I didn't know how to pay the electricity or my rent, and I mentioned this to my dad. He and my mom didn't know how to help me from afar, so he said, "Why don't you call your real estate agent?"

"Good idea."

So I called Rachel, the broker who had found me the apartment, and told her my problem.

"What?" she said. "I got you the apartment. That's my job. We're done."

But Rachel, who became one of my best friends of all time, held my hand through the whole process while I learned to do the adult task of paying my monthly living expenses. She never questioned whether I spent all the money that I earned. That *really* wasn't her job.

Now, going over a year of my finances with my parents, I was so embarrassed. I made more than most adults in America and I couldn't even pay my taxes, let alone put money down to buy a house or into a savings account. (It was a minor miracle that I did wind up being able to pay my taxes that year. Out of desperation, I called my agency to see if I had any money coming in that I didn't know about. That's when I learned they kept a "reserve fund" that they didn't mention and which they collected interest on. I cashed in my portion, which was just enough to pay my tax bill.)

You might have thought that was the wake-up call I needed to grow up.

Nope. I still had the feelings of invincibility shared by so many teenagers, and mine were blown out of proportion because I was a model, living alone in New York, and making a lot of money. My parents couldn't help me (and maybe that's why they didn't even try). This was something I needed to learn on my own. I thought that no matter how badly I messed up, I could always fix it. No matter how much money I spent, I could always make more. But that wasn't necessarily true.

I learned that when I missed a flight to a shoot because I didn't wake up when my alarm went off. I raced out of my apartment and into a cab, but when it quickly became clear that I wasn't going to make the flight, I had the taxi bring me to my agency. I told the cab to wait for me, left my luggage in it, and went upstairs to the offices, where I told the head of my division how I missed the plane.

"Why?" he asked.

"I overslept."

The agent—the same one I had to bother on a Sunday when I wound up in the hospital from drinking too much—leaned closer to me.

"Is that alcohol on your breath?"

I had been out with friends the night before, but all I had was a few drinks. Tequila. It was enough for him to smell it on me, and I had missed my flight. . . .

"You are not professional!" he yelled. "You miss your flight. You come in here with alcohol on your breath. And now you expect me to book you a new flight and take care of you when you can't even take care of yourself? I don't want you at this agency. You can't be at this agency anymore. Good-bye."

From the look in his eyes, I could tell he wasn't playing. I had to leave. Immediately.

On the cab ride back to my apartment, I was freaking out. My crying is not silent. The driver looked pretty nervous. As soon as I got home, I called my mom and dad, and through hysterical sobs told them what had happened. We had a long, honest conversation about my issues. They all revolved around responsibility, and my not taking it.

Upon the advice of my parents, I called my agent and apologized. It was a hard call to make, but everything I said was one hundred percent true. I told him that I wanted my career. I really wanted it. Modeling was something I saw for myself in such a bigger way than just living in New York for a year.

"I just want you to be better," he said. "I want you to want this as much as I see this for you."

He accepted my apology. I was very, very lucky. And that was it—the wake-up call I needed. I hit bottom, I guess. Now, did I stop drinking? No. Did I stop partying? No. I was just smarter about it. I didn't miss any flights from then on out. (To this day, I haven't, which I'm very proud of.)

I grew up that day in my agent's office in the way you do when you see your whole career and, in a way, your life flash before your eyes. I was always a hard worker—that's just how I was raised. It never mattered what the job was; a job is a job. If people have asked for my services, I wanted to give them nothing short of excellence.

I slowly learned that leading the party-girl lifestyle was not conducive to career success—particularly in my line of work, where you have to look and act the part. Everything shows on the outside for a model. If your eyes are puffy from lack of sleep or your midsection is bloated from a night of drinking, you aren't going to take great pictures.

It took a little longer for me to grow up financially, but after a few years I got there, too. As I worked harder to make sure I was giving my agents, clients, and photographers my best for their work, I began to take myself more seriously. That meant not blowing all my money on designer bags and being unwilling to read a subway map. It also meant wanting more from my career than just booking the next job.

I was in Montreal around the end of 2010, on a job for Canadian plus-size retailer Addition Elle, when I had an epiphany. Plus-size undergarments are the most frustrating thing in the world. For the most part, they are purely functional and come only in basic colors. And oh, so matronly. You've heard of mom jeans? Think mom bras. Constantly on the hunt for sexy, frilly, lacy bras and panties, I'd find the biggest sizes regular lines offered and stuff myself into them. It wasn't ideal, but it was better than wearing granny panties.

Why shouldn't curvy women get to wear lingerie that's every bit as beautiful as for women who are straight-size (the industry term for non-curvy women)?

At the time of the Montreal shoot, I had been working

with Addition Elle for about four years, but the company had a relatively new vice president, Roslyn Griner, with whom I got along brilliantly. During our lunch break on set, I sidled up to Roslyn and told her my vision.

"I want to do something really exciting," I said. "I'm going to start a lingerie line. I thought you should know in case you guys wanted to jump on this and do it with me."

Wow. I couldn't believe what I had just done. I'd pitched a fashion exec! To launch my own line! As a model, I was scared. Taking the initiative in business dealings was uncharted territory for models. You don't do anything without an agent; they have to be by your side. I always thought it was an agent's job to do everything for me. But sitting right in front of me was the chance to do something bigger than just booking a job. I didn't want it to slip away, so I decided to seize the opportunity to run my idea by an executive whom I liked and respected.

"What kind of lingerie would you want to make?" Roslyn asked me.

"Sexy lingerie, like this," I said, lifting up my shirt to show her a very intricate black lace Wacoal bra that I had found in the largest size they made and yet was still spilling out of.

"That's really beautiful. Okay, let me take this idea to my design team and we'll talk."

It didn't take long for Roslyn to come back to me with a yes.

She told me that Addition Elle was ready to get on the phone with my agent to work out the logistics. This was amazing news . . . except that I still had to tell my agent about the idea. I was a little nervous about how he'd react to what I had done. I had really stepped outside of the box. Some agents don't want their girls to make any moves without consulting them, which is understandable. Negotiating and contracts are tricky business. Models need to respect an agent's role and skill set—that's why they have agents in the first place. At the same time, I believe that we have the right to take initiative and go for what we want in our own careers. You can overstep, but you can also be too submissive. Luckily, my agent was happy that I had made the initial contact with Addition Elle, and supported my vision. He brokered the deal for me, just as he did with every other client.

What a deal it was! It was so much fun to go into Addition Elle with all my favorite pieces of lingerie—as well as photos of stuff I liked but couldn't find to fit. I loved the design team. They totally got me and created a lacy, racy French boudoir–inspired line made of lace and microfiber, so you can just throw it in the wash. Brilliant!

The first collection, which launched in 2013, didn't generate much profit but was an incredible learning process. I came to understand that you can't just make what you want; you have to make what the customer wants. This might sound obvious, but when you are creating clothing, you have to learn what is going to sell and what women are going to respond to. You have to learn price points and comfort levels. It takes a while to get things right.

The lack of profits out of the gate didn't matter, though, because Addition Elle was playing the long game with my line. We had so many goals for where it was going that we learned from our mistakes and moved forward—quickly! In 2014, the Ashley Graham Collection reached more than $1.6 million in sales. In 2016, it was up to nearly $4.6 million. The financial success has been gratifying, of course, but even more so have been the personal messages I have from women. So many different types of women write me all the time to rave about how sexy and comfortable the collections are. Even men write to thank me for creating lingerie that makes their wives feel so confident.

My own lingerie line was pivotal to my career not just because of how much money it makes or how much it has raised my public profile. When I took matters into my own hands that day with Roslyn, something profound shifted within me. I realized that all the agents in the world couldn't do what I can do for myself. When I stopped relying on others to do my job for me, that's when my career *really* began.

People respected me for the lingerie line, which brought me an enormous amount of credibility. I was no longer just a pretty girl but a businesswoman, with the numbers to back up my abilities. My successful line at Addition Elle led to a line of bathing suits with Swimsuits for All and another of dresses with Dress Barn—both are top sellers.

When a shoot is over, so is a model's work. But not mine. When I go home from set, I do my emails, work on my vision boards, research what kind of styles I want to see on my body. I am not looking for the next job. I am looking for the next opportunity to build my empire.

I'm also proud to report that I'm not squandering the

money I'm earning from these opportunities. Having realized how fortunate I am to do the work I do, and to be paid what I get paid to do it, I began to take serious stock, using financial advisers to plan ahead in the smartest way I can. I know my time in this profession is short. I also need to honor myself for working so hard, and that means treating the money I earn with respect.

chapter 5

Taking Cover

Good enough for the "fat girl" is not good enough for me or you. Take charge of your own destiny by claiming it.

I was in Texas in the spring of 2010, on my way to do a catalog shoot for JCPenney, when I received this text from my friend:

"Your boobs are all over page two of *The New York Post*."

"What???" I texted back immediately.

He replied with a picture of me in the red, lacy bra I had worn for the recent Lane Bryant commercial, with a headline proclaiming, "Banned-ad model: ABC is a big bust."

Filming my national commercial had been one of the highlights of my career. In the clip, I am trying on a bunch of frilly bra and panty sets and frolicking in a gorgeous mansion until I get a reminder on my phone to "meet Dan for lunch." So, like any girl would, I slip a trench coat over my red bra and panties and, with nothing more on, head out for "lunch." I'm no Meryl Streep, but I had so much fun acting in that commercial.

The ad, though, had been banned from running during prime time viewing hours by both ABC and FOX, which is why the *Post* had done a story in which I was quoted saying, "I was very surprised. [ABC] can't handle bigger on TV, bigger boobs on a normal-sized woman on TV."

The networks had a different story. The reason they provided for banning the ad was that the commercial was too risqué. Sure, it was full of innuendo (ahem, "lunch"), but within the context of television's contemporary landscape, my Lane Bryant spot was pretty harmless, if not kinda cute. So what was really going on here? What were those networks really reacting to? The "girls" (aka my boobs).

Nobody ever told me this directly, but it became obvious to me that in the minds of network executives, a size 16–18 woman in lingerie was just too much to show during family hour. As I told the *Post,* Victoria's Secret had ads featuring its angels in much skimpier lingerie and in much more compromising positions all over prime time, so it was my shape that made me overtly "sexual." Nobody told me this was true; I was just going off my own experience as a woman. When I went through puberty and got curves, I immediately attracted male attention. And the bigger the curves got, the more attention I got.

If you put a model who doesn't have much boob, butt, or hips in the tiniest bra and underwear, she can still appear—I don't know—girl-like, fashionable, artful, I guess. But take voluptuous women like me, and put us in any type of lingerie . . . and we're immediately thrust into the amazon category. The curves of our bodies. Everything is just *out* there in full view.

There's a lot of cultural theory by people way more educated than I am about the cultural and sexual implications of the female form, whether thin or thick. Throughout history, a bigger woman signified wealth, desirability, and fertility. In more contemporary times, we are beaten over the head with the notion you can't be too skinny or too rich. Twiggy might have been the first model to turn thin into a brand, but that brand has been carried on for years now by straight-size girls, from Kate Moss to the majority of models you see on runways or in magazines. They may be cool and high fashion, but does everyone think they are sexy?

I'm always perceived as more sexual than straight-size

93

models. Maybe it's because my boobs are bigger. I don't know what it is. My theory is, I'm just damn fine.

When word got out about the Lane Bryant ad being banned, news outlets all over picked up the story. I got a call from my agent, who said, "This can be your moment." He was being inundated with requests for interviews with me. "This can be what takes you to the next level."

While I was overwhelmed by the situation, my mom was thrilled about it. She thought I looked beautiful in the ad and wasn't the least embarrassed by it. The only advice she and my dad had for me was to listen to my agents.

As it turned out, the only piece of advice I received from my agent was to "just stay positive." That was the sum total of my media training! (And that's all I've ever had, to this day.) I had never even given a single interview in my life, but I just told myself over and over, "Okay, I got this. Be positive."

And I was, and it turned out to be really good advice. I stayed positive everywhere I appeared, from National Public Radio to *Good Morning America* to *The Tonight Show with Jay Leno*. I also spoke my mind, questioning the logic behind why it's so offensive to see a size 16 woman dancing around in lingerie on a commercial airing during *Dancing with the Stars,* where the majority of women also dance around in close to nothing. The only difference is that the contestants on that show wear single-digit sizes.

I'll be honest: I pulled a lot of what I said right out of thin air. I'm the queen of "fake it till you make it." All those years of charming my teachers into giving me passing grades was useful for something.

My only misstep—or more accurately, the one comment my agents didn't like—was when I said something along the lines of, "America's getting bigger, and that's why plus-size models are actually becoming a part of the norm." But my agents did not want me to go there. "We don't want to get into the obesity issue," they told me. "You're not an expert. You are just a model."

They were right. I'm not an expert in demographic shifts or the obesity epidemic in our country, so I decided to stay in my lane—fashion—which is why I put up a huge fight when I was forced to wear a dress by a mass retailer for whom I often worked when I did an appearance on Jay Leno's show around this time. Instead I wanted to wear a Narciso Rodriguez dress that took me two days to find. A black, ribbed, body-conscious, classic black dress that went just over the knee, I had it tailored and everything. It felt so perfect, but I was told there was a client who would never hire me again if I didn't wear their dress. I didn't like having my career dangled over my head or the dress the client picked, but I wore it and just snatched it really, really tight. Nothing was going to ruin my appearance on *The Tonight Show*!

What I went through is hardly different from what many curvy women experience every day. Oftentimes we aren't able to wear what we really want. In my case it was because of work, whereas usually the limitations have to do with the minimal selection in bigger sizes and being pigeonholed with false labels about our style because of our shape. If you're a big girl, you might have to wear a plus-size clothing brand that doesn't have exactly what you are looking for. But just like I did with the dress I wore on TV, make it your own—particularly by tailoring the garment to show off your best asset. As I always tell anyone who will listen, "Tailoring is your best friend."

My agents weren't wrong: the controversy over the commercial ban put my name out there in a big way. I started getting recognized by women in the airport, on the street, on the train, everywhere.

"Oh, you're that plus-size model." Or, "You're that one in the lingerie." This didn't happen often, but enough that Justin, whom I had started dating, said to me, "I'm so glad I met you before all of this happened, because we wouldn't have been able to date the way we did if I hadn't."

My day rates also went up thanks to the controversy. As a familiar face, I was more desirable. Wanting to capitalize on "my moment," I came up around the time with my idea to start my own lingerie line for women like me. On the heels of the ad controversy, I felt this was my chance to create something great, important even. People might not have remembered my name, but they knew my face—and they associated me with lingerie. I was already a plus-size lingerie model, but now I was officially the Plus-Size Lingerie Fashion Model.

I also started to reconsider the idea that I wasn't the kind of model who appeared on the cover of or inside fashion magazines.

Early on in my career, I was in awe of my friend Crystal Renn because of the high-fashion work she booked—

editorial spreads in *V* magazine and French *Vogue,* the cover of *Glamour,* where she appeared in a bikini alongside Alessandra Ambrosio and Brooklyn Decker. When Crystal became the first ever plus-size model in a major high-end fashion campaign, the modeling agency threw her a huge party, that's how big a deal it was. While celebrating with her at the event, I asked Crystal how much she'd been paid for the campaign, thinking it would be in the hundreds of thousands of dollars. I won't say what the fee was, but let's just say it was way less. Way, waaaaaaaay less. It was so little that I didn't understand why she had even taken the job. "To catapult me into the next thing," she replied. Crystal was very smart about her career. She always had a bigger strategy in mind. She wasn't just focused on the day-to-day. In this she was different from most models, including me at that time.

A few days later, I repeated that conversation to my agent. I knew I was lucky because I had a steady stream of work for catalogs and campaigns for large retailers like Target and Lane Bryant. But I asked my agent what he thought about my taking some less-lucrative, more-high-fashion jobs in order to raise my profile.

"You know what, Ashley? At the end of the day, Crystal may be my star," he said, "but you are my money girl."

It didn't make me mad at the time. It pissed off Justin, who was convinced from the start that I shouldn't limit myself to being only a catalog girl. I, however, took it as a constructive criticism—which, as my dad taught me from an early age, was the only way to get better at whatever I did—

and I kept it moving. Looking back, though, my approaching him about doing editorial work was trying to do my job "better." I wanted to expand the scope of my abilities but was shut down. According to my agent, I was the fat happy girl and should remain that. "You aren't a cover model," he said.

The real work of an agent is to get you an invitation, while it's the model's job to get invited back. In this framework, you're at the mercy of an agent's perception of where you belong—in other words, where you should be invited. As with any close relationship, they might have your best interest at heart, but that doesn't mean they share your vision.

I wanted more, but this was years before the commercial ban and the lingerie line. I wasn't yet the confident person I am today. Instead of rebelling against my agent or even finding a new one, I decided to be more dedicated than ever to becoming his "money girl." If that was the definition of success for me, so be it.

I followed my agent's guidance and focused mostly on catalog, swimsuit, and lingerie work—although there was one high-end editorial opportunity that came my way. I couldn't believe it when my agency said I was on hold (the industry term for when a client blocks time on a model's calendar but the job isn't yet confirmed) for what would certainly be my biggest shoot up to that time, the June 2011 issue of *Vogue Italia*. Steven Meisel, the crème de la crème of fashion photographers, was shooting the cover spread. The only plus-size model he'd shot before was Crystal Renn in *Vogue's* Shape issue. Pat McGrath (whom *New York* magazine called "the most in-demand makeup artist in the world") was doing the makeup, and they'd gotten Guido Palau for hair (he broke out styling the biggest supermodels of the '90s for George Michael's "Freedom!" music video and has been creating iconic looks ever since). As a model, this is where you wanted to be—no ifs, ands, or buts about it.

Every single plus-size model I knew went on the casting call, which was at Steven Meisel's studio in New York's SoHo district. The elevator opened right onto a small waiting room where about ten curvy models were already crowded in when I arrived. When it was my turn, I walked into the big, open, airy loft and was greeted by Steven and Pat, both sitting on a couch. They were friendly and kind, but not in a fake way. Smiling and asking me a lot of normal conversational questions (like where I came from), they seemed excited about the shoot.

Having never shot an editorial in my life, I was awed in the presence of the stardom. I had taken two hours to get ready—to look like I hadn't gotten ready. I can't tell you how hard it is to do no-makeup makeup. Going against my own grain (I love a lot of bronzer, mascara, eyeliner, and eyebrow pencil), I felt so vulnerable in the casting. But, as I said, they were very nice and loved my modeling portfolio.

When I debriefed Crystal later, she reinforced my confidence. I told her Steven had been so nice to me, and she said, "He's hard to read, but I have a really great feeling about this for you!"

"Do you think he saw my Lane Bryant commercial?" I asked. This was right after the ad ban and the notoriety that went with it.

"Honestly, probably not, because he's Steven Meisel," she said. "But you never know."

The night before the shoot, I received a call from my agent: "Hey, I just want to let you know: You've been released."

"What?"

"They ended up going with four girls instead of five."

I was the only model who didn't make the cut. Devastated and dejected, I cried. (I was eating pasta to celebrate what I thought was a confirmation on *Vogue Italia* when I took the call and remember weeping into my spaghetti after I got the bad news.) I couldn't believe it and was so confused. How had I missed what I believed to be my only opportunity to appear on the cover of *Vogue?*

This experience threw me for a loop for a long time, particularly because I never found out why I didn't get the job. Models usually don't. (It didn't help that people kept confusing me with the models who *did* make the cover: "Were you that brunette I saw on the cover of . . .") Justin always reminded me, "It wasn't your job to have. You get the jobs that are meant for you. This one was meant for them. Your jobs are your jobs and theirs are theirs." He was right, but the rejection was still painful.

I worked hard not to resent the other girls, and the easiest way was to convince myself that what my agent had said to me all those years earlier was true: I'm not an editorial girl. My destiny is to be the happy-smiley catalog model for Lands' End or Kohl's, or the sexy lingerie girl for Lane Bryant or Bare Necessities, I told myself. And that's fine.

I was resigned to that concept of myself and my career for a long time. But a few years later, I took my career in my own hands. I launched a lingerie line, and everything changed. It was as if God heard my prayers—and answered them—as soon as I decided not to follow what others decided was best for me but what I wanted for myself. And that included getting my first cover on a major fashion magazine.

The whole thing unfolded so naturally. A stylist who'd worked with me on one of my Addition Elle campaigns was a big fan, so she presented to the editors of *Elle Québec* the idea of doing a cover with me—and they went for it.

I knew that a big part of the reason I got the cover of that magazine was because of my lingerie line and the publicity it had generated in Canada, and as I headed to the shoot in Cabo San Lucas, Mexico, I told myself this was the best business move I could make. This was only going to raise the bar for me again and lead to more contracts. I was the money girl.

I didn't know anyone from the crew who would be at the shoot in Cabo, and I didn't really know what to expect. Naturally, I had worked out a lot leading up to it, because I knew I would be photographed in a bathing suit. Well, the shoot turned out to be amazing. With my hair all wet and in my face, it was very *La Dolce Vita* à la Cabo. The photos were so beautiful and I had so much fun.

But the truly mind-blowing experience was when the cover came out in June 2014. It wasn't until I saw my image that it hit me: I had never in my life thought that I could achieve this. I had been told that I would never be on the cover of a magazine and I had proved to that agent and any-one else who told me to stick to catalog work that I could be on a cover. But, most important, I proved to myself—when I saw how amazing I looked on *Elle*—that I was indeed a cover girl after all.

You know how powerful it can be when you discover that you can do something you never thought you could? It changes everything . . . and gets you thinking about what else you can do that you weren't aware of.

Still, a year later, when IMG, the modeling agency I had recently joined, suggested I go out for the *Sports Illustrated* Swimsuit issue casting, I was doubtful. "I'm a big girl," I said to my new agent. "Why would *Sports Illustrated* want a girl like me?" The iconic Swimsuit issue wasn't even on my radar. I honestly never imagined it was even a possibility for me.

"We don't know what'll happen, but we want you to go," my new agent, Mina White, told me.

That's what makes a good agent in the modeling world; they will pitch you even to clients who aren't asking. Later on, Mina pitched me to other big magazines, fashion week castings, and huge companies that had never even seen a curvy girl. But first Mina called over to *SI* and told them that she was sending over to the casting a "really sexy, curvy plus-size model we want you to meet. Just be open to it."

That's how I found myself in front of MJ Day, the edi-tor of the Swimsuit issue. She picks every model you see in its pages. A fellow curvy girl, MJ and I hit it off instantly. We had a great conversation in her office, which was then in Rockefeller Center, about how our physical body type

Already posing in front of the
camera in a bathing suit.

I have always loved my mama.
Look at her beautiful smile.

At four years old I had
nailed my go-to pose.

It's true that my bathing suit love
started early.

My dear grandpa,
who taught me so much.

My trusty Victoria's Secret bikini.
Gosh, I loved that thing.

Rocking cutoffs and tube socks in
the magic kingdom.

During this phase I looked an
awful lot like a boy.

Early test shots. Can you believe I'm twelve years old in this picture?

This is one of my first
catalog shots. Plus size clothes
haven't changed much.

When you're getting
started, you never say
no to a job.

I started working
internationally very early
on. Here's an ad for a
German clothing catalog.

These were my favorite pants in the
eighth grade. I probably wore them once a week.
Gotta love '90s fashion.

Ah, New York—where reaching for the heights of fashion is only natural. Opposite, a sweetheart neckline edged with beading adds romance to this ivory crepe empire-waisted gown with poet sleeves and chapel train, about $700, by Venus. Also available in white and dark ivory. Pearl and crystal tiara, $435; matching drop earrings, $113, both by Fenaroli. Crystal sandals, $78, from Special Occasions by Saugus Shoe. Menswear and shoes by Gingiss. This page, enjoy the freedom of an ivory strapless satin gown with embroidery, side pleat detail and chapel train with rhinestone trim, about $420, by Jessica McClintock. Also available in white. Silver, 18K yellow-gold and pearl earrings, $65, by Hilary Drusman. Silk satin slingbacks, $130, by Grace. Menswear and shoes by Fubu. Men's 18K white-gold ring, $1,585, by Jose Hess. For more info, see page 649.

563

I was a fifteen-year-old bride (catalog model).   I loved working for JLO.

Me at fourteen.

Two of the most important people in my life—LeOra and John Friesen.

A great family vacation in Hawaii
with my mom and sisters.

Hangin' with my mama on our Brooklyn rooftop.

Early days, when Justin and I were dating. He snapped this pic in a cab.

My posing partner Crystal Renn.

The happiest day of my life. With my brand-new husband,
Justin, and my oldest friend in the world, Rachel. And that dress was killer.

Justin's thirtieth birthday party. He makes me smile every day.

isn't represented in media. The Swimsuit issue is no exception. The images of the most beautiful women in the world, sprawling on exotic beaches, wearing pretty much nothing, really mess with women's heads. You just feel bad about yourself while flipping through its pages, because you know you'll never, ever be that. I told MJ all about my lingerie line, promising to send her some pieces as soon as I left her office, and that was that. As sure as I was that I wouldn't be in *Sports Illustrated* when I went into the casting, that's how confident I was when I left that I *was* going to be in it.

Walking down Sixth Avenue, I thought about how my dad used to get *Sports Illustrated* delivered to the house when I was in middle school. Those were the Christie Brinkley years, and my dad told me in no uncertain terms, "She's the most beautiful woman in the world."

"Yeah, she's pretty."

"Her smile is what makes her," he said. "You have to smile anywhere you go. Smile, smile, smile."

"Okay, Dad."

The memory and the meeting with MJ had me smiling now. I called my agency and said, "Let me know when *Sports Illustrated* puts me on hold," as if it were a done deal.

Ha ha!

I didn't get it.

It wasn't the first time I had been wrong, but I was just as upset as I had been when I got dropped from the *Vogue Italia* cover shoot. It felt like a door had been slammed in my face. Well, as it turned out, I was wrong about that, too.

What happened next, literally the very next day, was

that Mina called to say I had a confirmed job with a company called Swimsuits for All. This in itself was not exactly earth-shattering news. Working for clients like this retailer that carried swimsuits in all sizes, including plus, was my bread and butter. However, *where* the company decided to place this campaign, called #CurvesinBikinis (in which I wear a little black string bikini while a guy in a full suit falls into a pool at the sight of me, naturally)—now, *that* was groundbreaking.

The marketing geniuses at Swimsuits for All had decided to take out a prominent (and I'm sure extremely expensive) ad in the *Sports Illustrated* Swimsuit issue. The investment was worth it, though, especially when Swimsuits for All released the image of me to the media right before *SI's* big cover reveal on February 2, 2015. The news of my ad appearing in that magazine completely overtook the press. It was *everywhere*.

> *"Joining the ranks of supermodels Kate Upton, Heidi Klum and Chanel Iman, Ashley Graham will now grace the famous pages of* Sports Illustrated's *iconic Swimsuit Issue—and she's making history."* **—PEOPLE**

> *"Everyone's talking about the* Sports Illustrated *Swimsuit Edition, like we do every year. But there's one new TWIST this year: There's a plus-sized bikini model in an ad in the 2015 issue."*
> **—USA TODAY**

"Larger-than-average model Ashley Graham, 27, will break the bikini ceiling."

—NEW YORK DAILY NEWS

There was tons of press, everywhere. Press, press, press, press, press. *Entertainment Tonight,* CNN, the *Today Show,* local news, national, and everything in between. My publicist told me I was the number one most-googled person that day. The breathless way in which many outlets reported the story obscured the fact that I was in an ad in the *Sports Illustrated* Swimsuit issue, not the editorial pages. They also ignored the news that the Swimsuit issue actually featured a plus-size model.

Sports Illustrated may not have yet been ready for my size hips and breasts in their editorial pages. They put a model considered plus-size in the magazine, but at six-two she looks more athletic than curvy. As I told the *Daily News,* "I really hope this opens up doors for not just skinny girls with big boobs, but for girls with big hips and thighs."

And that's exactly what it did; the interest my ad garnered proved to *Sports Illustrated* that putting a woman of my size in its pages was going to make news, and that the news was overwhelmingly positive. So when I went back for my second casting for *SI* in the early spring of 2015, I was sure this was the year they'd put me in the magazine. MJ was so happy to see me again, and felt that my ad was exactly what needed to happen to create the kind of change we had talked about a year earlier.

But again I didn't hear anything. I kept waiting and waiting for that call. By my birthday on October 30 I had given up hope, because it was my understanding that by the end of that month *Sports Illustrated* stopped shooting for the Swimsuit issue. I gave myself the pep talk that models know so well (because we have to give it to ourselves all the time). It didn't matter. Better things were in store for me. Blah, blah, blah.

Then came Thanksgiving, where I was just in a "Screw it" frame of mind, and ate two full plates of food. By that point, I had given up all hope. It was anything goes when it came to food, and the gym was just a place down the block I visited once in a while. The week after the holiday, my agent called to say that the modeling agency was doing an internal, day-in-the-life video of a model to show executives and they were going to send a camera crew to follow me around for the day.

"I'm getting a colonic and a facial," I said. (I sometimes do colonics to make sure my stomach isn't bloated before a shoot and to keep my tummy feeling good on the inside. What I've been told about colonics is that they help you stay healthy since they flush harmful bacteria.) "It's really boring stuff that I have going on today."

"It's fine. They're just going to come pick you up."

The crew came to my apartment. "So, guys; guess we're hanging out today," I said.

In the car, the producer started asking me about being in *Sports Illustrated* for Swimsuits for All last year, questions I had literally been asked a million times. I went on autopilot, answering without thinking. "It was amazing for the industry. . . ."

Our first stop was the agency itself, where I was signing an exciting new contract with Dress Barn for my own dress line. While this was certainly a big deal for me career-wise, I had already reviewed the forty-page contract in detail. All that was needed now was my signature and then I'd be on to my next appointment. I figured I'd be at the agency fifteen minutes, tops. Twenty if I stopped to chat.

When I walked inside the huge, open lobby of the agency, a number of people stopped their typing, and everywhere I heard, "Hi, Ashley!" and "How are you, Ashley?" and "Oh, Ashley! It's so good to see you!"

This was not typical, but I figured that the staff, usually in their own little worlds, were just being extra outgoing for the cameras. But things only got stranger from there. When I arrived in the office to sign the contract, there were about twenty people waiting in the room. *Huh?* Then I was informed that the president of IMG worldwide, Ivan Bart (a seriously important person in this company and amazing human), was on Skype from Paris, apparently for a meeting happening after this. *Okay?*

Sliding the contract over to me, Mina said, "You have to initial every page." So I started initialing.

"Ashley, read the contract," she said.

"I already read it last night," I said, as I kept signing and flipping and signing pages.

"Ashley!" she said, slamming her hand down on the desk. "Read the first lines of the contract."

"Okay, sheesh. I don't know why you are being such a jerk about this."

She apparently really wanted me to read this contract that I had already read, so I flipped back to the front and read the first words:

"*Sports Illustrated* Swimsuit Model Contract."

I took a moment to process what I was reading and then immediately burst into tears.

"Is this real? Is this real?"

The crew caught the whole scene on camera, my ugly cry, Mina's tears, everything. I had made it, curves and all, into *Sports Illustrated*. The pages, not an ad.

The first person I called was Justin and the second, my mom. She was in a movie, so she didn't answer the first time. But I had to talk to her, so I called again, and because she's a mom, she was worried something was wrong and left the movie to call me back.

"Is everything all right?" she asked.

"Yes!" I said.

"I'm in a movie. I'll call you when it's done."

"No, you can't. I have to tell you something really exciting."

As soon as I told her, she started to cry. This meant almost as much to her as it did to me.

That was basically all the celebrating I had time to do. You'd think they'd give the new girl a little time to prep for her shoot, but no! I had my shoot, the last of the whole issue, the week after I signed my contract—two weeks after Thanksgiving. Terrific.

There's only so much you can do in a week to prep your body for a swimsuit photo shoot. I started by cutting out sugar so I wouldn't be bloated or have any acne. I also had another colonic two days before the shoot, because I always truly believe they make my stomach flatter. They do sort of make your stomach flatter . . . but only if you're really bloated. And they don't make fat disappear. I worked out a little bit harder, but not much.

I didn't go crazy at the gym or dieting, because I figured the folks at *Sports Illustrated* liked the way I looked at the casting, so why try to alter anything? It wasn't like they didn't know what they were getting. You can't change your body for a moment or an event, like getting married. I'm all for making lifestyle changes based on long-term goals or health decisions. But if you diet or exercise just for a date or a high school reunion, you will never be happy with the results.

Before my *SI* shoot, naturally, I got the darkest spray tan of my life. I mean, I looked like a burnt sweet potato. When you are on the beach, the water reflects light off your body so that in photos you look lighter. If you are modeling swimsuits on the beach, you want to looked bronzed, because it's sexy. The woman who gives me my spray tans comes to my apartment and hoses me down right in my kitchen. Then she baby-powders me all over, and I go to bed covered in grease and powder, because you have to sleep in the tan before you can shower. (Justin always knows that it's hands off on spray-tan nights. . . . Can't have any palm prints on set the next day. "Spray-tan sheets," he says. "Got it.")

My best shot at looking good for my *Sports Illustrated* photos was to do what Crystal Renn had taught me early in my modeling days in New York. I bought an old *SI* Swimsuit issue and flipped through it, looking at different positions and poses. Then I got in front of my old friend the full-length mirror and mimicked the poses to see if I could make them work for my body shape. Being a curvier, bigger girl, I have to think about a lot more than other models do; certain poses just aren't flattering.

The prep I did in front of the mirror was better than any starvation diet, because at the shoot, MJ instructed me "not to think about swimsuits. I want you to think fashion." I was on a beach in a tiny string bikini, sweating my butt off, trying to make sure my boobs look good, my stomach was flat, and a million other things, but I had my marching orders: fashion!

So I put my body into a position I had practiced, which I called the Emily DiDonato, after the famous model—on all fours, with my butt up a little bit and boobs pushed forward. Emily and I had shoots that overlapped on one day, and I told her how I'd named my sexiest pose after her. She loved it and thanked me. Anytime I have the opportunity to empower another model, I take it.

That pose turned out to have a lot more impact than even I imagined. It wasn't until the *Sports Illustrated Swimsuit 2016 Revealed* special, which aired the day before Valentine's Day, that I fully understood.

Hosted by Nick Cannon and Rebecca Romijn on TNT, the live special was a pageant-style show specifically to announce the newest *Sports Illustrated* cover girl. While they were showing montages of each model (and the countries where we'd been photographed), all the models were waiting backstage. There were girls *everywhere*. Because this was my first time doing *SI,* I was pretty overwhelmed. Were my strappy sandals cutting into my ankles? Did my boobs still look high and lifted? (Because my motto is, If your tits aren't high and lifted, what's the point of life?) All these deep thoughts were running through my mind when suddenly I had to pee, so I started for the bathroom, only to be stopped by a guy in a black suit and headset. "Where are you going?" he asked.

"I have to pee really quick."

"Can you just wait one second?"

"Do I have to?"

"Yeah. You have to."

You don't argue with a man in a headset, so I went back to my spot among the throngs of models backstage.

Only a few minutes later, another man in a headset appeared. He escorted Hailey Clauson, a blond model with full lips and long legs—the classic bombshell *SI* girl—out of line; then he took Ronda Rousey, a mixed martial artist, the first American woman to earn an Olympic medal in judo, and a model in the Swimsuit issue; next he came for me. Confused, I saw that the president of IMG, Ivan Bart, was standing nearby with my agent, Mina. Between the lights, music, and wall-to-wall models, there was so much going on that I didn't have time to process why Ivan and Mina had tears in their eyes as they stared at me.

The man in the headset then took Hailey, Ronda, and me toward the front of the stage, where the hosts were preparing to announce the cover girl. My brain immediately put

|||

the pieces together. There was no way they were giving the cover to Ronda, because she's an athlete. The cover girl is always a model. And they definitely weren't going to give it to me because I'm the fat girl. I was lucky to be in this magazine at all. Logic dictated that Hailey was the cover girl, but they were bringing Ronda and me out for the reveal because we were groundbreakers. I told myself the usual, that just standing next to this year's *SI* cover girl while she got the news was going to be great exposure for me and take my career to a new level.

Soon the three of us went out onstage. Standing between Ronda and Hailey, I excitedly whispered to Hailey, "You got the cover! You got the cover!"

As Nick Cannon started to amp up the energy, getting ready to announce the big news, I was awed by the moment. I could feel the combination of luck, hard work, and God's grace all at once. Who knows how I got here? I thought. However it happened, I'm taking it.

Nick Cannon took a quick look at all three of us, and then he shouted to the live audience, "Never before! Three different covers for *Sports Illustrated*!"

Boom! Enormous red curtains fell from three towering magazine covers of Hailey, Ronda—and *me*.

How could this be? I'm the fat girl.

But it did happen. The proof was right behind me in a larger-than-life image of me doing the DiDonato. There I was, in a small, purple string bikini, my hair wet and brushed over my face a bit, and a wave smacking my hip—a *Sports Illustrated* Swimsuit issue cover girl.

The image was as new to me as it was to everyone in the audience. As a model, you never get to choose your photos, so, honestly, you never know if you are going to like them. You always hope and pray that they'll be good, particularly if they are as high-profile as a cover, but as Mina once told me, "Bad covers happen to good people." *This* was a beautiful cover.

Hailey, Ronda, and I looked at each other, still confused. We had expected things to go as they always did, one cover, one model, end of story. Nick immediately asked each of us for our reactions. Ronda offered an upbeat and measured response about this being an exciting time. This is a woman who takes punches to the head; she wasn't going to freak out about being on the cover of a magazine. Hailey was poised and perfect, saying exactly the right thing about being grateful to be part of such wonderful diversity. And me? When Nick asked me, "How do you feel, Ashley?" my body just kind of took control as I yanked the mic out of his hand in one swift motion and said in my loud voice, "This is amazing! I'm gonna take over!"

I'm going to take over?

Why I said that I have no idea. It just came out of my mouth. Yet, no matter how random or seemingly absurd, all words have power. When you get a *Sports Illustrated* cover, your life changes. That's it: forever, you're a *Sports Illustrated* cover model. I knew this was my moment. *The* moment. But that meant it was also time for a lot of others just like me. For so long, the magazine only had one look, one type of beauty—and that goes for color as well as size. (Tyra Banks, the only African-American woman ever to appear on the cover of *SI*'s Swimsuit issue, called me when I got my cover to say, "You are making history, just like I did.") My cover proved that beauty comes in all shapes and sizes. There is no one standard for gorgeous.

When I said I was going to take over, I knew I was taking a lot of women with me: all the curvy women in the world who didn't feel they could be prom queen, CEO, girlfriend, or cover girl, all the girls who say, "I am the fat girl." Well, guess what?

We are taking over.

chapter 6

How to Slay Your Style

Fashion can come in so many shapes and sizes and styles. But for that to happen we need to stand up and make our voices heard, because the people who make clothes don't know what we want. We have to tell them.

I don't care how big my hips and boobs are, or how high the number on the scale is, if my waist is snatched, I know I look good.

I've felt this way ever since my body developed. As I've said, I hit puberty around twelve years old, and boom, I was a woman. Or at least looked like one. I don't know if I inherited my self-esteem from my mother or if I was born with some kind of innate confidence, but instead of hiding my newfound assets under baggy clothing, like many girls who develop young tend to do, I went in the opposite direction.

Case in point: the outfit I chose to wear for my first day of eighth grade. We had just moved from Texas to Nebraska, so this was a totally new school. Because I'd already lived in five different states by this point, I felt like I had to prove myself at each new place. You would think I'd be used to it by then.

All I know is that I walked into that Midwestern school wearing leopard capri pants, a really tight, thin, noodle-strap black tank top that showed my bra, and black platform sandals. It was quite an introduction to middle school. I was five-nine, totally curvy, with a butt and boobs, flat stomach, big curly hair. I had painted my nails red and covered my face in way too much foundation and blush. Even in eighth grade, I was really into makeup, and my mother was a willing accomplice. Every time Clinique had a special, my mom would take me to the department store and we'd get a bag filled with the newest products, as well as all the freebies they'd throw in. And she'd let me wear *a lot* of it. My going to school with my belly and boobs out, with red nails and tons of blush, didn't conflict with my mom's value system. I guess she felt my heart was in the right place, even if the buttons on my shirt weren't. (My dad, on the other hand, hated the way I dressed. One time when he told me to button another button on my shirt, I replied, "That's not the way the shirt's supposed to look." Because I knew instinctively that a longer neckline made my upper body look smaller. But my dad wasn't too interested in getting a fashion lesson. It infuriated him, although I'm not sure what made him angrier—my attitude that he didn't "get" style, or the style itself.)

I didn't wear outfits like the one I did for my first day of school to be provocative. At least not consciously. That was just my style. I was obsessed with the Spice Girls. No, I *was* a Spice Girl. If Ginger and Scary Spice had a child, it would have been me. I wore leather skirts, knee-high socks, and my hair in two topknots like Baby Spice.

While I wasn't necessarily trying to be sexy, a big part of fashion for me has always been about figuring out what part of my body I want to show off. Maybe that's because, as a curvy girl whose body type hasn't historically been represented in the pages of fashion magazines or on billboards, I had to put more thought than my thinner friends into how I wanted to represent my body in clothes. It might be just the leg with a high slit up the thigh or my breasts in a low-cut shirt, but no matter what, whenever I get dressed I purposefully think about what element of my body to highlight. It doesn't have to be just one element, either. It might be everything. Actually, a lot of times, it is everything. When I won a contest at my first modeling expo in Nebraska, I chose a white tube-top dress to wear when collecting my prize. It was so, so tight. And white. And I couldn't have felt more confident. I love that Mattel decided to clothe the Barbie that they made to look like me in the Opening Ceremony dress I wore to my lingerie fashion show. You don't get more form-fitting than that dress.

Now, I wear tight clothes because that is my style. That's what I think I look good in and so I feel good in them. But I don't think there is any one rule to dressing curvy women. The problem with plus-size fashion, in general, is that there are so many rules put on us. To me, thinking that all curvy girls need to wear tight clothes is just as false as thinking we need tents to hide in. Both are limitations for women, who all are built differently and look so different.

Fundamentally, I think a curvy woman's style should be based on her comfort level and desires. Unfortunately, it's not always easy for us to find clothes that we think look hot. What comes to mind when you think of "plus-size" fashion? Oversize T-shirts with childish graphics, baggy jeans with bedazzled butts or bell-bottoms, empire-waist dresses with cutesy bows so it seems like the designer confused "curvy" with "pregnant." Cheap fabric covered in animal prints, unfortunate smatterings of glitter and sequins. If you've ever shopped in a plus-size store, you know what I'm talking about. It's just sad.

As a curvy model, I've seen every kind of bad fashion. So many clothes made for larger women have details, such as oversize prints or random bows, that make them look even *larger*. And I have worn a lot of doozies in my career, but the worst outfit I've ever had to model was a sweater that featured a dancing cat and bells (real ones) and camel-colored corduroy pants. Oh, yeah.

The thing is, I'm not just a model for larger-size fashion; I am also a consumer—and generally speaking, I'm not happy about my experiences when I go shopping. First of all, there's an overall lack of inventory. I've been living in this section since I was a teen, and let me tell you, shopping for prom or homecoming was the worst. Apparently, only older women are size 16, because it was always a struggle to find a dress that was sexy, youthful, *and* big enough. The only dresses that fit me were matronly tentlike things I wouldn't be caught dead in.

As a curvy girl, you get the feeling that in the world of fashion, you're a second-class citizen. Consider the placement of plus-size retailers in the average mall or department store. They're often hidden away behind the furniture section, on the bottom floor or some equally hard-to-find spot, as if we curvy ladies were trying to buy a dirty magazine instead of a blouse. Or they're next to the food court, as if being thick means you can't make it a hundred feet without eating. Whether you're forced to shuffle past Subway or a bunch of sofas to get to your clothes, it can be pretty darn soul crushing.

Curvy fashion blogger Corissa Enneking described the disheartening experience of trying to shop in the plus-size section of a major retailer. At first she was "impressed" that there were actually larger sizes in the store she visited, because, though more and more retailers are getting into the business of making clothes in larger sizes, often they don't bother to actually put them in stores. Online shopping has vastly expanded options for larger women, but it's not fair to exclude us from the brick-and-mortar experience. We want to try things on too, you know.

Despite Corissa's initial excitement over the existence of a plus-size section at the store, ultimately she found the tiny area badly lit, poorly stocked, and in complete disarray; in a word, "horrifying." That prompted her to write directly to the clothing chain to "take the time to treat us with the respect and dignity that you treat your other customers. . . . Create spaces that make people proud to wear your clothing. Bring positivity into your stores, instead of alienation." Corissa hit the nail on the head.

It's crazy that we are treated like second-class citizens, considering just how large a market we represent to the fashion industry. The CDC puts the average American woman at size 14, but research out of Washington State University that was published in 2016 says that statistic, based on twenty-year-old data, is way out of date. The average American woman now wears between sizes 16 and 18.

Just as our sizes are getting bigger, so is our appetite for shopping. The plus-size apparel market in the United States has outpaced the overall apparel sales market from 2013 to 2016—by *a lot*. According to independent data from the market research company The NPD Group, the plus-size clothing market rose a whopping 17 percent in that three-year period, to account for $20.4 billion in sales annually.

That's compared to a 7 percent increase for overall apparel in the same time frame.

Those increases in sales are all the more remarkable considering that most designers refuse to create clothing bigger than size 12. According to a 2016 analysis by *Bloomberg*, only 16 percent of the dresses on JCPenney's website were size 16 and above. The higher-end the fashion line, the lower that percentage gets. For example, on Nordstrom.com, only 8.5 percent of the dresses offered were plus-size.

It can't be that the fashion industry doesn't like money. So what's the problem? Tim Gunn, fashion guru and Emmy-winning cohost of *Project Runway,* wrote, in an extremely popular op-ed for the *Washington Post,* that he finds the industry's attitude toward curvy women "baffling." And unacceptable. "Many designers—dripping with disdain, lacking imagination or simply too cowardly to take a risk—still refuse to make clothes for them." And millions of women just like me stood and cheered.

Designers say that creating clothes for women above size 14 is more challenging. Variations in proportions grow with size, so this is true, as designers can't necessarily just scale up from a smaller sample. For plus sizes they need to create more patterns.

It is a little bit more challenging to make clothes for bigger bodies. You can't just take a piece of silk, drape it around a form, and call it a day. Some women have back fat, thick stomachs, huge breasts. Designers really have to consider structure, fabric, straps, and support for us.

Where it gets really complicated, however, is that while no two bodies are the same, when it comes to curvy women, our differences in shape are even more pronounced. I think that's the most beautiful thing about being in this community; no one is the same. In general, all women are unique, whether it's our hair texture, skin color, bust, or shoe size. None of us *can* be the same. Yet we in the curvy world are the ones who have had to confront and accept that truth, even when designers and manufacturers still haven't. We don't have a choice. One size 16 gal might be wider across the hips and have a tight waist, while another is graced with great girls and a flat butt, so the same size 16 will not fit her the same way. Our curvy diversity in shape and size means that designers have to be more innovative and more creative with what they put into the plus-size market.

What it all boils down to is that if you're a curvy lady, you have to work a lot harder to be fashionable. I know I'm *incredibly* fortunate that I have not one but two stylists who help me look good. And even so, sometimes I still have no idea what to wear. Putting an outfit together can be intimidating. But I have learned so much from my years of experience in the industry and watching both my stylists in action.

My personal stylist, who dresses me for interviews and everyday events, is a fellow curvy girl. Although she's shorter than me and her boobs are a lot smaller, she tries everything on when she shops for me, because it gives her a gauge of whether it'll fit me or not. More important is that, though we're shaped differently, she gets the whole aesthetic of being a curvy girl who also wants to be fashion-forward. She dressed me for the whole first season of *America's Next Top Model* and slayed every single look!

For big events I use another stylist, who creates super, high-end, luxe looks for me. Having dressed A-list movie stars for so long, he's grateful now to have a curvy client like me, because it's proven to him he "can dress any kind of woman." His biggest goal for me is highlighting the hour-glass curves of my body. Whatever it takes. I'm confident in his hands, because he never wants me to look matronly.

I certainly wasn't matronly when he dressed me for the 2016 GQ Style Awards in London. He put me in a Tadashi Shoji gown, but first he took off the sleeves, removed the high-necked collar to leave only the lace-detailed bodice, created a thigh-high slit, and cinched the waist with a belt. One headline accurately described the result as "Ashley Graham puts on an eye-popping display."

My high-end stylist did similar tweaking to a Moschino dress I wore to the Harper's Bazaar Icon event. There was the thigh-high slit, the cinched waist, and the deep-cut bodice. He also removed the leather sleeves from the black leather bodice and spray-painted the bright-blue skirt! What's most incredible about that was that it was a couture gown designed by Jeremy Scott and handmade in Paris. Just for me. And still, my stylist went to town to make it work after he saw it on my body.

The moral of the story is, even with a specialty item as fancy as that, you need to make it your own. Nobody, not even the most talented designer or stylist, knows your body better than you.

That's why, when I went to Turks and Caicos in the Caribbean for my first *Sports Illustrated* Swimsuit shoot, I brought a bunch of bikinis of my own with me! Okay, the people who work on this issue have hundreds of bikinis— and I brought *my own*. That's how worried I was that they weren't going to have any that fit me the right way. I'm a 36DDD, and I need some major support up top. These girls are not sitting under my chin, if you know what I mean. I was so worried that the *SI* stylists weren't going to come up with tops that were going to . . . well . . . hold me up.

Once I got there, the fitting was a breeze, mainly because I know my body. I told the stylists, "The bigger the bikini, the bigger I look; the smaller the bikini, the smaller I look." After they saw me in some of the high-waisted bikinis they had brought for me, they totally agreed. So we twisted the extra material up on the sides, and then I held it lower down on my hip, manipulating the originally old-fashioned-looking bikini bottom into something decidedly more modern and flattering.

I shot in fourteen different bikinis that day, as well as a couple one-pieces, and the stylists thanked me for livening up all the swimsuits. "These bathing suits that we thought were going to be boring look incredible on your body, because of your bangin' curves," they said. "Thank God for your body because otherwise this swimsuit would be boring." I mean, there's only so much you can do with a bikini. And the best thing is to fill it out or up.

They weren't being condescending. I could tell it really had been fun for them to work with the new shapes my body presented. I'm glad they appreciated me—and my bathing suits. In my *SI* rookie photo (that's the term they use for a model's first picture in the magazine), where I'm lying on my back, I'm wearing a purple-and-black bikini I brought from home!

Yes, we curvy girls need to work harder. Always. When I got my wedding dress, I really had to be smart about it and strategize. Part of my problem was that because Justin wanted to get married so quickly, I didn't have time to special-order something made just for me. But I couldn't find anything off the rack in my size that I liked. I was at my heaviest during my engagement, a full size 16/borderline 18. My hips were 48 inches, which technically made me an 18, but everything else was a 14–16. The whole size issue was semantics, because the dress I found and fell in love with was a 10. The champagne-colored, strapless gown had a bustier-style top that laced up the back and a full, billowy skirt with tiers of large ruffles. In addition to removing all the bedazzled diamonds and extra-long train (I'm not *that* over-the-top), I had all the seams opened up, and the corset bustier was on the loosest setting possible. I don't know how it worked out, but it did. My boobs were overflowing to the point where when I sat down they just went, *hoof*! And I did feel a little self-conscious sitting across from Justin's older, more modest-minded family members (some of whom I had just met) with my chin resting on my boobs. But what can you do?

I know I looked good, and fundamentally that's always my goal. I consider myself a fashionista. Of course I do. But, more specifically, I want to be that fashionista for the curvy girl at home who also aspires to look amazing no matter what the number on the label of her pants says. While I may not be protesting in front of city hall for cleaner water or anything like that, I do consider myself an activist of sorts. Let me explain what I mean.

Even after I moved past the catalog world and started landing more mainstream work, I found myself trying to squeeze into sample sizes. Getting a size 16–18 body into a size 4–6 sample size dress? I'm a model, not a magician. Because there was such a lack of high-fashion clothes that fit my body, many stylists were forced to do what I call the old "diamonds and panties" look.

If you look at the *Vogue Italia* cover featuring plus-size models, the girls are essentially naked—not just on the cover but throughout the entire spread. All they have on are diamonds and panties.

That's one solution to a lack of high-fashion clothes in larger sizes. Another is what they often did when they shot *Vogue*'s Shape issue. You'd see a curvy model wearing a dress, but it would only be halfway on, slipping off her shoulders, while she held a breast or something. That's because magazines don't think the clothes made in our sizes are cool enough (they are right), and the high-fashion clothes they like don't come in our sizes. The other option is for editors to choose the type of plus-size model who can fit into straight-size clothes (meaning a size 10 who can squeeze into a size 6, even if it means not zipping the garment up the back) and just make her look bigger or more voluptuous.

Those options provide opportunities for curvy girls to appear in high-fashion settings, and I'm all for that. But it does nothing to prove to designers that there's a real need—both in department stores and in the pages of *Vogue*—for larger-sized clothing.

Because of this, while I will always shoot half-naked (I have to), I have drawn a line for myself. I will not show nip and bush. I did it a couple of times before, but never felt truly confident with my decision. Part of what happens in the high-end fashion world is that when a photographer gets a curvy girl in his or her sights, all he wants to do is shoot her naked. The way the lines of her hips and back fold into each other, the softness of her thighs—it's gorgeous to a photographer's eye. It's also exotic in the world of fashion—a medium always looking for the new—in that you just don't see it often. And when you do see it, it is beautiful.

When I refuse to be shot completely naked for high-end fashion editorial jobs, I am making a statement: "Don't just shoot me naked. Find clothes that fit me."

I assume that when a photographer or magazine hears my policy, I will be released from a job. But I've never been told that to my face, because that's not how my business works. Overall, though, I think my being confident and outspoken has gained me more in the industry than it's caused me to lose.

I'm not the only curvy woman who is speaking up. Many others just like me have voiced their desires for better-fitting, cooler clothes, and because of that demand there have been some significant changes in the plus-size apparel landscape within the last two years. There are *a lot* more clothes available. Many mainstream brands like Old Navy, Forever 21, H&M, and others are doing fashion looks in size 16 and above. They aren't doing this out of the goodness of their hearts. The plus-size division of ModCloth doubled in 2013, making it the fastest-growing part of their business and prompting the online retailer to add one hundred twenty-five plus-size designers to its original team of thirty-five. Sales for Eloquii, an online plus-size retailer with trendier looks, saw its sales grow by more than 165 percent in 2015!

That's great, but there's still a lack of quality clothing for curvy girls. You can get great trendy pieces at Mango or ASOS, but you can't get most of what you'd find on Madison Avenue or in *Vogue*. There are a few high-end designers, like Prada, Gucci, and Vivienne Westwood, that occasionally go up to European size 48 (our 18). That's still not big enough for a lot of curvy women, and usually you have to special-order pieces in that size anyway. When designers actually design up to size 22, many buyers for department stores and other retailers won't order anything larger than a size 12, because they believe larger sizes don't sell.

The excuse often cited for this lack is that the plus-size consumer doesn't want to spend the money for clothes made by designers of this caliber. The problem is more complicated than that, however. Take PLY Apparel, a high-end luxury line for curvy women that launched in 2013. Women used to Lane Bryant prices get sticker shock when they see $850 skirts and $1,300 gowns on PLY's website. Meanwhile, the upscale retailers where those prices are the norm won't give PLY's designs a spot in their stores. So the consumers who are in that bracket and that size are not likely to be reached.

I love a great Gap or Target shopping spree as much as the next girl, but for my size 16 sisters, I really want high-end clothing as well. It's the principle. It shouldn't be okay for designers, who can make whatever they can dream up in their heads, to keep larger women out of their clothes—or for buyers to tell us how we will and won't spend our money.

I've faced this kind of prejudice, even as a successful model. I was once on hold to be in a runway show for a really, really big-name designer. They ended up not booking me, though, because they said they just didn't have the means to make me a dress. I was confused. Every single dress on a runway is custom-made. So they were making custom size 2 dresses for their runway models, but they couldn't make a custom size 14 dress—that might make women feel good about themselves? It's simply a double standard.

I was really angry about not booking that gig, because the runway is a testament to what's ahead for the next season. So, if you're putting curvy women on your runway, it's tantamount to saying, "This is the type of woman who should and will be wearing my clothes."

Granted, some designers have put curvy women on their runways. Singer Beth Ditto walked for Marc Jacobs. Jean Paul Gaultier had two plus models in his shows. So did Mark Fast. For 2016 New York Fashion Week, Christian Siriano put five curvy models in his show. Still, it's not yet the norm.

Maybe it's just an old-fashioned mindset: this is the way it's been, so this is the way it's going to be. Change is hard. It's going to take special people to step outside the boundaries of what's historically been deemed acceptable.

But there's no better place than fashion to set a new trend. I would think this community would jump on the opportunity to create clothes for curvy women—not only because they'd reach a whole new (and significant) customer base but also because it's a chance to imagine new forms of beauty.

Until that day comes—and it will come—you should feel free to go into *any* store you like. Even if you know for sure a boutique doesn't carry your size, that doesn't mean there isn't something in there that fits you or that you can't find inspiration for ways to put together your own looks.

Now, I know it's not as simple or easy as that. We curvy women can be treated like a redheaded stepchild when we walk into certain stores. And by the way, so are a lot of straight-sized women. Fashion can be cruel if you don't have the "right" skin color, economic status, cultural background. . . . There's a lot of work to be done in the industry.

Actually, I had such an experience very recently. I was going around London with a journalist who was writing a piece about me for a top British fashion magazine, and we wound up in a very high-end English department store. Perusing pieces from Valentino, Roland Mouret, and other top designers, I found a Balmain skirt I wanted to try on. From previous experience, I know that Balmain fits me; in fact, I often wear a size 12 in their clothes.

I approached a salesperson, holding the skirt up.

"Do you have this is in a forty-four or forty-two?" I asked her.

She grimaced like I'd asked her if they had the skirt with vomit on it.

"No. No, we definitely don't have that size," she said, not even offering the consideration of walking to the stock-room to check.

"You don't?"

"No, we don't."

The sad part is that my initial reaction was to think about *the writer*! I was sure that the woman interviewing me, who couldn't have been bigger than a size 2, had never been body-shamed to her face like I had. Basically, I didn't want her to get embarrassed *for* me. Often skinny people, who feel for their bigger friends, don't want us to be called fat because they don't want us to feel bad. Where I'm coming from, though, is that I have been called fat most of my life. I'm much better equipped to handle the situation than they are. I didn't want the journalist with me in this moment to feel like she had to stand up for me. I know how to stand up for myself.

I went into mean-girl mode, which is a self-defense mechanism of mine. If you're going to treat me like garbage, I'm going to treat you the same way. But then, what good does it do?

I rolled my eyes, turned on my heel, and started to walk away. "Oh, my God," I said to the writer, loud enough to make sure the saleswoman could hear.

Some other people on that floor must have known who we were, because the rude saleswoman was called to the back. While we were still browsing the racks, another clerk came out and approached me. "May I help you?" she asked in the most solicitous tone. When I told her what I was looking for, right away she said, "I'll be right back," only to return, sure enough, with my size.

See, it doesn't matter if you are a well-known model on an interview with *Vogue*. Body shaming knows no boundaries. That's all the more reason anyone and everyone with a curvy figure should feel emboldened to ask for what she wants.

When I first moved to New York, my first question in a store was usually, "What's your biggest size in here?" If they answered that it was 10 or 12, I'd say, "Thank you. Goodbye." And then I'd just leave.

What I've realized, though, is that that wasn't just insecurity doing my shopping for me but a bad sense of fashion as well. Once I got a little more confidence, I figured out that sometimes I can squeeze into a 12 (I've *even* squeezed into some 10s), and it just fits me a little bit differently. Now, I'm willing to try on sizes that I didn't think that I could ever make work. What's the worst that can happen? You can't get the zipper up? From Paris to Brooklyn, I've gone into places where I know they don't have my size, just to look around. It's still fun.

My closet is a testament to the truth that size is relative. I have items that range from 8 to 18, because every designer cuts differently. Believe it or not, I even have some "smalls" in there.

I have the *Sisterhood of the Traveling Pants* closet. Literally. Friends and family of all sizes are always digging around in there and always find something fabulous to wear. Once, when my sister-in-law and I were going out to an event, she arrived at my apartment, complaining, "I have nothing to wear." So I just start pulling dresses out. My sister-in-law, a size 8, wound up looking stunning in my electric-pink Alexander McQueen dress with a high neck and no sleeves.

Of course, my clothes look different on her than they do on me. There's a little black dress I got from ZARA about eight years ago that she wore just the other day. On her, it was a little bit longer and not skintight, but it still looked great. Whether you're a 6 or a 16, my motto is, Who cares? You'll always find something in my closet that fits!

I predict that in the next five years, max, we curvy girls will have anything and everything we want. I mean, you can't satisfy 100 percent of the people 100 percent of the time. We may not have as many plus-size models on the runway as we'd like, or designers might continue to cut armholes too darned small. But we won't be stuck shopping in the basements anymore, either.

However, the change starts with each of us. If you want to be fashion forward, and you're curvy, you have to be open. Trust me. Just try it on.

chapter 7

I Feel Your Food FOMO

There is no magic bullet for figuring out the right food for your body. Everyone's system is different. The secret is learning what works for *you* and not worrying about what anyone else says or thinks.

The pasty green beasts taunted me from my plate. They were sickeningly wet-looking and slightly puckered around the edges from being overboiled by Mom. Lima beans. Yuck. A dreaded enemy food, and although they were the only things left on my plate, there were a lot of them.

I looked over at my sisters, who had smartly folded their lima beans into the mashed potatoes to disguise the taste. Me? I'd just shoveled in the buttery potatoes without a thought. Then I ate my chicken and a few soft dinner rolls, washing it all down with a big glass of iced tea. I was full. The only problem was, in our house, you finished what was on your plate. No ifs, ands, or buts.

"What's wrong with you?" my mom said. "You're not eating."

I looked up at my parents, who ruled over our dinner table—by that I mean, over what my sisters and I ate. There was always a starch (or two); meat (either a piece of beef or chicken); and a green. Some nights my mom would switch it up and we'd have something exotic like gumbo or French dip sandwiches. But we sat down together for a complete meal every night—and you were expected to eat every single morsel presented to you. When we were little, they made the plates for us. As we got older, though, we had to take a little of everything, and, of course, eat it all.

We would get a spanking if we didn't finish what was on our plates. (After the spanking, you still had to return to the table and eat.) One time my sister had to sit at the dinner table for the entire night, because she refused to eat the two green beans left on her plate. My dad wouldn't let her up until those beans were gone. My pile of lima beans was never going to fly.

"You're not going to finish those?" my dad asked, pointing a threatening fork. I hated lima beans, but I hated being spanked more. Slowly, I choked them down.

And so began my long, complicated relationship to food.

I'm not a parent, but when and if I do become one, I'm definitely not going to force my kids to eat everything on their plates. I don't believe in waste, and I know children need to eat a variety of foods. However, there are other ways to teach good eating habits. I know that my parents meant well. For them it was a health issue. They honestly thought that well-balanced meals, as they conceived of them, were crucial to our growing up healthy. But making me finish everything on my plate developed a mindset that I carry with me to this very day.

It's 100 percent ingrained in me never, ever to leave food on my plate. It doesn't matter how big the portion I've been served is or how stuffed I am. Those last fries from an enormous pile—you know, the ones that have grown cold or soggy in ketchup—they call to me.

And don't talk to me about leftovers. Tricks like immediately splitting your food in a restaurant and asking for half of it to be wrapped up to go—that doesn't work with me. In its to-go container, the lasagna emits a sonar message telling me to eat it before I get home. It's not surprising, since that's what my family would do when I was growing up. If we took food home from a restaurant, my mom would start eating it in the front seat. My sisters and I weren't far behind her.

"Can I have some?" "Yeah, can I have some, too?" This was right after we had just had a whole big meal. "Sure," she'd say, and like that, the leftovers were gone.

Growing up, a lot of the culture of our family life revolved around food, and not much has changed. If nutritionists have some kind of chart with all the symptoms of overeating, I'm pretty sure I'd hit each one.

Use food as a reward? Check! Again, this started young. "You'll get an ice cream if you clean your room!" my mom would say. Chocolate for folding the laundry; dinner out at a restaurant if I got a single A on my report card . . . So food has always been a strong incentive for me. It's terrible—to this day, I still reward myself with food. I'm constantly trying to change this motivation that drives me to food. But if I work out every single day for an entire week, my first thought is, "You can have pizza and Pinkberry tonight for dinner."

I've heard that good habits lead to other good habits. Not so when it comes to me and eating. I was so good for the three weeks before the New York Fashion Week runway show for my lingerie line this year. Really, what choice did I have? I was about to strut down the catwalk in a bra and panties. Of course, there is always a choice. . . . I didn't eat any dairy, because of the bloating, or any "bad" carbs like pasta or bread. No desserts. Just veggies, lean protein, etc. And I worked out four or five days a week. There was that *one* minor slip-up the night before the show where I ate lobster fried rice at my good friend's birthday party. Still, for me that's good. Very good.

So what did I do after the runway show? I ate three pizzas in one week.

My rationale for this indulgence was that I didn't have a runway show to prep for anymore, and I had done such a good job—so I really deserved to give myself a treat, or three.

The reality is, though, that models always have something to be ready for. Obviously I don't believe in starving yourself for the camera, but a little restraint does go with the job. A photographer like Mario Testino or designer like Marc Jacobs could call up out of the blue and say he wants to shoot you tomorrow. And then what? You've just eaten three pizzas, that's what! So I'm supposed to keep myself in check. I should do that not just because I'm a model but because I'm a human being. Moderation is a healthier lifestyle than the highs and lows of food reward and withdrawal. That's just common sense, right?

There's only one thing keeping me from a permanently well-balanced diet, and it is another one of my major issues: food FOMO. The Fear of Missing Out. It might sound funny, but it has a big hold over me. I can be anywhere, *anywhere,* and it'll come on. Any city I travel to, I have to find out what they are known for there, and the best place to get it, because I feel like if I don't have this food in this place where it's famous, I'm missing out on an experience I may never have again. (Meanwhile, I travel all the time.)

When I last went to Paris, I decided I had to have foie gras every single night. In case you don't know, foie gras is made from duck or goose liver that has been intentionally fattened. So, basically, it's the fattiest, richest food ever created in the history of food. That didn't stop me from going on a foie gras tour of the city, which ended with me on the bathroom floor of my hotel room, vowing never to touch another piece of liver as long as I live. You'd think that'd teach me, but next time I'm in Paris, I'll probably do the same thing.

Ashley's Culinary World Tour

In Italy, I have to have gelato every day.

In Sweden, the candy is the best I've ever tasted, so I buy it in bulk!

South Africa's exotic meats—ostrich, boar, shark, and buffalo—are to die for!

Dubai has some of the best hummus I've ever tasted!

I'm a sucker for rice and beans in any part of the Caribbean.

Any time I go to the South, I find the new "it" mac 'n' cheese place!

I'm also obsessed with the raw and vegan restos that pop up all over LA. Delicious food doesn't have to be unhealthy.

It isn't only when I travel—FOMO can hit me anytime I go out to eat. Even if Justin and I are at a mediocre restaurant grabbing a quick bite, I want to try everything, not only on my plate but on his plate as well. Just to know. Just to taste. That's how deeply rooted an issue this is with me. Justin hates it when I eat his food. "I'll give you my heart, my kidneys, even the clothes off my back," he says. "I just don't want to have to share my food with you."

"Then you married the wrong woman," I say.

That's not the last of my issues surrounding food. I also have portion control problems. My eyes are always bigger than my stomach—and if it's on my plate, well, going back to my first issue, I'm going to finish it. The result is a lot of stomachaches.

The night Justin took me to a fancy Italian restaurant for my birthday is a classic case. No sooner had we walked in to Il Mulino, a famous restaurant in the West Village, than I ordered a dirty martini. Why? I have no clue, because I never do that. But there was something about the romantic, candlelit interior and waiters running around in formal black jackets, starched white shirts, and white bow ties that made me feel like I should be fancy. It was my birthday, after all.

As I sipped my very strong martini, one of the waiters came over to our table with an assortment of cured meats and bread and the biggest hunk of Parmesan cheese I have ever seen in my life and began shaving off huge pieces onto a plate. That was just to enjoy with our drinks. They hadn't even brought out the menus yet!

We ate everything that night: pasta, meat, fish, cheese (so much cheese), and dessert. While drinking our postmeal liqueur (this was on top of the dirty martini and wine), Justin revealed his big surprise.

"We're driving upstate! I've rented a cabin for us."

"When?"

"Right after dinner. It's your special birthday getaway."

My heart sank. Here he had done this wonderful thing.

"My stomach hurts so badly. I can't even believe I ate that much."

"Oh, no."

Poor Justin. How many times had he heard those words, "my stomach hurts," and then had to deal with the consequences?

I spent the whole first night of my special getaway on the floor of the bathroom. The dairy had an intense effect on me and it ruined our whole trip. There was nothing cute or sexy about me, because I had eaten too much Parmesan and pasta with heavy cream . . . and then dessert. It was terrible. (TMI, I know. Think of my poor, poor husband.)

The irony is that food gives me a sense of control, even though it makes me totally out of control. Food is something I can choose, order, have delivered—whenever I wish (especially in New York City). I sit down, eat, and feel really good in the moment. At its essence, food is nourishing. There is truth in that. The trick is understanding and respecting the line where it crosses over into something unhealthy. Unfortunately, most of us in America have been conditioned to believe that that invisible border is best defined by a diet.

Like so many curvy women—heck, like women in general—I have been on every diet that you can imagine. My first was Weight Watchers, when I was fifteen years old. I was already working successfully as a model, but I was also a teenager. I was gaining weight and decided I was fat. I wasn't, at all. I was just growing, but I decided to try to put a halt to it with a diet. Weight Watchers, a sensible weight-loss plan based on calorie counting, has helped millions of people eat better and lose weight. But for a dyslexic teenager, who hated school, counting of any kind was not something I was ever going to stick with. The method felt like a whole lot of homework that was way too complex for me. I prayed, "There's got to be something easier than this, God!"

And I never stopped looking for an easy way to lose weight. I did the cabbage soup diet, which is your classic, nutrient-poor crash diet. You can eat as much cabbage soup (made from cabbage, tomatoes, green peppers, mushrooms, onions, and bouillon) as you want. Yay! Each day you get to eat something else—like bananas and milk on Day 4, beef and tomatoes on Day 5—but not much. If you can stick with it all week, of course you'll lose weight. This diet cuts the average person's calorie intake in half. Plus, cabbage is a natural diuretic, so you also lose a lot of water weight. I lost weight on the cabbage soup diet but felt terrible. I was hungry, weak, and, at times, sick. I pretty much gained back any weight I had lost right away. Oh, and I don't even want to talk about the gas. I'm not sure anything is worth suffering cabbage gas.

The cabbage soup diet was one in a long line of weight

loss attempts, including juicing, Atkins, and the Master Cleanse. You name it; I've tried it.

Meanwhile, I'm married to a man who, when he's full, easily pushes his plate away and says, "I'm done!" It doesn't matter if half the food is untouched.

Grrrrr.

Not only is he tall and naturally lean but if he wants to cut bread out of his diet, he just tells himself that's what he's going to do, does it, and moves on with his life. I don't get it. I can't cut anything out of my diet; I am not that girl. If I am going to modify my diet in any way, it takes so much focus and determination that it quickly starts to feel like a second job that isn't worth the lousy pay.

Whether it was from experimenting with various diets or the yo-yoing back and forth with occasional overeating, I started to develop gastrointestinal issues, and eating was immediately followed by bad stomach pains. (It felt like it was any food, but I later found out that dairy was the biggest issue for me.) It was so upsetting to have food, a source of great pleasure in my life, become associated with pain. While weight has plagued me over the years, I never lost my love of eating. So this new issue was really upsetting.

I didn't have the patience to slowly cut one item after another out of my diet to figure out if there was a single cause for my stomach issues. Staying away from dairy didn't take away my problems. I applaud people who can do things like that, but to me it feels like a full-time job. And I already have a job. I ended up hiring a food combination specialist. Food combination diets, like the Zone, are based on eating foods in certain combinations that will not only help you lose weight but are also better for you. At this point, I was hoping for the latter.

"We're taught to eat the heaviest food in the morning and then slowly go lighter as the day goes on," the specialist told me, "but that's all wrong." Her method was to go from eating foods, such as fruit, in the morning that are easier to digest, since you're eating on an empty stomach. For lunch, have a small protein with a green *or* a starch—but never the three together!

"But that's how I was raised," I said.

"Yeah. I know," the specialist replied.

Dinner is where you can kind of go big: a juicy steak and a good glass of red wine, or a big bowl of pasta (as long as it's rice-based). Her entire method, in the end, was no less complicated than if I had done an elimination diet to see if there was one food group causing my stomachaches. Instead I reached out to an expert to guide me, which makes anything much easier. In the end, the diet did make me feel better (the original goal) and I lost a bit of weight (not bad, either). Even better, though, was that I learned more about myself, which is what happens whenever you experiment with your routine.

Food combining worked for a while, but then my body changed again and it no longer worked. I didn't start having stomachaches again, but my body was less receptive to this way of eating. That's what happens with any restrictive eating system: your body plateaus (at least mine does). Plus, my lifestyle was getting in the way of eating lightest to heaviest.

If I got off the plane in Germany and I was starving and had to go straight to a shoot, there was no way I could survive on a piece of fruit until my next allotted mealtime.

Like I said, I did learn from the experience, so it wasn't all for nothing.

I started eating a little more moderately. Now I'll have a couple of eggs with avocado and toast or a protein shake in the morning. Lunch is usually whatever is fast and easy, but never compromising my no-fast-food rule. That stuff is just gross. Dinner is always a piece of fish or meat with a starch and veggie, or whatever my hubby decides to cook. I can't cook (I'm *almost* the perfect woman).

My big realization on this round of my long learning-to-eat-right journey is that I had to start eating more often throughout the day, with less on my plate each time. I know this is not rocket science. Most people with lifelong good eating habits do this very thing without even thinking about it. But when something doesn't come naturally, it takes longer to get there. Focusing on good ole portion control—not OD-ing on food or finishing everything on my plate, no matter how heaping—has definitely helped me break my old habits, and feel better, too.

I'm simply not able to adhere to strict rules around deprivation when it comes to food. I'm going to eat what I want. Just not as much of it. There are weeks where I am really good about making the right choices. And trust me; there are weeks where I eat everything I want, in not such a good way. But I no longer carry such a heavy sense of guilt, because I feel I've found a good balance for most of the time. This is the key—eating the right way most of the time, but allowing myself to indulge some of the time, is realistic for me.

I still have my days where I wake up and feel so fat because I ate a whole pizza the night before. Everybody has those moments. (Mine are particularly bad when I go back to Nebraska. It's really hard for me to eat healthy there. At home in New York City, in any four-block radius, there are tons of healthy choices from salads to green juice to sushi. Back home, they don't have such great options in terms of grabbing a quick bite, and I regress. Swaddled in a big sweatshirt, I return to my adolescence and all that means— including bad eating habits. Such as an undying love for French dip sandwiches and my mom's candy bar dessert, which is layered peanut butter, Rice Krispy treats, and milk chocolate, all melted and hardened in the fridge. I can eat the whole pan.)

Now, at least, I don't feel as bad about it when I really indulge. I'm not constantly beating myself up when I eat something I really love, or a little too much. I know how to get myself back on track, whether it's working out a little harder the next day or going right back to my routine of eating well.

Eating and working out are inextricably bound together, for good and for bad. Although working out makes me feel really good, it lacks the easy, instant-gratification quality of food. Hitting the gym can also give you the false sense that it's okay to overeat—basically canceling out your workout.

But when everything's in equilibrium, nothing beats sweating it out for both mind and body.

However, too many of us curvy women feel like they aren't welcome in the gym. That's why I love getting my butt kicked at Dogpound. You wouldn't think the trendy gym in Tribeca where Victoria's Secret models work out could be a warm and welcoming place. But it's one of the friendliest gyms I have ever been to. Everyone who walks in (not just models) gets greeted with a high five or a hug. If you haven't been to the gym in a couple of weeks, the staff checks in on you by text. It's a family atmosphere where everyone is training hard.

There are other reasons some curvy women avoid the gym. It can be because there aren't other women who look like them, they don't feel like they know what to do, or there simply aren't great workout clothes to fit us. In general, I'm a black-on-black girl, but in the gym I like to go a little crazy with my palette. I like to wear bright colors like a neon-colored bra and shirt, and printed pants. If you are size 16 or bigger, however, it is very difficult to find active-wear that fits properly. If you find some that fits, it's usually so cheaply made that when you bend over you can practically see through the fabric—and it loses its shape as soon as it goes through the wash. As with other areas of curvy fashion, there is simply a lack of quality, which is so unfair. Walking into a gym alone can be intimidating for a big girl. Adding a bad outfit just seems cruel.

The game changer for me was meeting Morit Summers.

It's been an incredible experience to have a female trainer who is not only amazing at what she does but is also my size. A big girl her whole life, she one day changed her diet, started working out, and found her life's work. Although she remained "bigger," she's solid as a rock.

What's interesting for me to witness is how people judge her ability because of her size. When one of my friends met her, he said, "I don't get how she's so big—and she's your trainer?" All I said was, "Look her up." He did and discovered she was the highest level of trainer at Equinox, a chain of high-end fitness clubs as well as a company that runs such hot workout brands as SoulCycle. It's no joke—and in the personal training division, Morit is on the highest rung. My friend was impressed and apologetic.

Morit is an excellent trainer who really kicks my butt. We do all kinds of weights, body resistance, and TRX bands. Obviously it depends on my work schedule, but I try to get to the gym at least three times a week, which presents a challenge because I easily get bored working out. So Morit always has to mix it up for me. Every day is different. However, there is one constant: you have to work out your butt. She's all about the butt. Your glutes are one of the biggest muscles in your body, so if you work that out, it's going to burn fat all day long. My butt and thighs are always a must, so no matter what, I know I'll be doing lunges, squats, or other booty-strengthening torture.

Now, I know I'm extremely lucky that I can afford a trainer and I know not everyone can. But the lessons I've taken away from working with Morit are ones anyone can follow. The biggest misconception is that the purpose of going to the gym is to *change* your body. We should be working out to be *healthy*. The idea of physical transformation can be so defeating for some women, because it is subjective (not to mention that people are overly critical when they look in the mirror). Even if your body doesn't "change" in the course of a year, it doesn't matter: your fitness level will.

I want women to know that no matter how big you are, you should always try to work out. If you are intimidated about going into a gym, follow an online workout at home. Or get a friend and go out for a walk. You've heard it before. It sounds corny and cheesy, but it works.

I don't think I have any special wisdom that nobody else can attain when it comes to diet or exercise. I see my evolution as a natural part of maturing. I have a greater understanding of my body and my relationship to both. When it comes to food, while I know that it still plays a big part in my life, I'm also not completely powerless against it.

Some Christians fast when they want to hear from the Lord more clearly. People can fast from food, television, social media, sex—whatever you feel is becoming your god in that it's lording over you. I've fasted from food before and found it challenging, but not in a way that was insurmountable. In some ways, I would even say fasting is a relief, because I didn't have to monitor what I ate. The whole equation was nullified.

Yes, the first few days are really hard. You just have some water and lemon and you keep it moving.

The bond between food and me is like other relationships in my life: complicated, evolving, demanding, and in need of constant work. But together we've come so far, moving from my childhood obligation to clean my plate, to a mindless need to fill up, to a truly nourishing and pleasurable exchange. That's the real reward.

chapter 8

The Ties That Bind

Building a strong foundation for a lasting relationship isn't always easy or fun, but it's worth it in the end.

In my life I often talk about how words have power. Whether it's formal prayer, giving a friend or loved one encouragement, public speaking, or writing down what you want on a vision board, I truly believe that the act of simply naming something has the ability to make it a reality.

For good or for bad.

For our fifth wedding anniversary, Justin took me to an exclusive, members-only restaurant in New York City where you have to ring a doorbell and say your name to be allowed to enter. If you're not on the list, you are not getting in. It was all very James Bond, 007. Justin always plans incredible ways to celebrate our anniversary. It's a very important event for both of us, and this was no exception. The place had such a cool and unique vibe.

In the private, dimly lit environment, we didn't talk about love or romance. No, for the entire anniversary dinner, we talked about what it would look like at this point in our lives if we were no longer married. It wasn't a sad or angry conversation. We hadn't been fighting at all. The discussion was purely a series of hypotheticals, along the lines of *What would you do? How would it play out for you?* The reality was that life had gotten so busy for both of us. And, along with the pressure of both our demanding professions, we essentially had a long-distance relationship.

Justin is a very talented filmmaker. His background is in documentaries, but he has worn various hats throughout his career, lending his vision and skill as a cinematographer and director for narrative works as well. Los Angeles is the heart of the film and television industry, so he made the natural decision to pursue the work he wanted to do in the place where it happens. Once he made the move out West, he quickly landed a gig as a cameraman for a successful television series based in LA.

I was thrilled at Justin's success, but if the center of his career is LA, mine is New York. I believe that when a model moves to LA, her career dies. Yes, there are the Kate Uptons, Emily Ratajkowskis, and Alessandra Ambrosios of the world, but those girls already had big names when they went to Los Angeles. While I had achieved a lot, I still didn't have the kind of confidence in my brand at this point that I would need in order to move to California.

Like all married couples, Justin and I have had our fair share of problems. Our first year of marriage was difficult in the normal way it is for most newlyweds. We were two people trying to get our unique and different rhythms in synch. Each consecutive year we grew more and more together. Growth is not always easy. Yet, as the years went by, our marriage became easier. Our story has the typical arc of a couple that loves each other, shares common values, and gets along.

Then came the fifth year, and it was by far our most difficult. A major source of friction between us was that Justin's work took him to LA too much for my liking. Justin could easily be gone for six months of the year, on and off, because of his work. Distance puts a strain on any relationship. We didn't have some special pass that kept us from the stress of being apart just because we love and support each other wholeheartedly. The work of managing all the moving parts in our lives and our relationship was overwhelming at times. We weren't truly contemplating splitting up, but it was hard not to imagine living as singles when our rhythms had become so independent. As wonderfully compatible as we are, Justin and I are also both very independent. Navigating our daily schedules solo feels as natural for us as being together. Sometimes when you get into your groove, it's hard to find room for another person.

The scary subject of divorce was also front and center, not just because of how our careers were putting us on opposite coasts, or because of our wedding-anniversary dinner conversation. It was also because my mom and dad, the last two people on earth that I'd ever thought would split up, had divorced the year before, and the fallout was still very fresh in our lives.

The end of their marriage was jarring for me not because I thought they had the best relationship in the world. They didn't. It was because both my parents were raised to believe that when you say your marriage vows, it means you're together forever, for good or bad. No matter what. My mother in particular had a deep faith in the institution, since her parents had a legendary marriage.

My grandpa John and grandma LeOra, who married when they were nineteen, were husband and wife for only a few months before my grandfather lost his arm in a corn grinder accident. After that my grandmother essentially had to become his partner in all the work of the farm, which is why my grandpa referred to his wife as his "right hand." LeOra maintained the home, and was also a farm wife, in the tractor, out in the field, hauling corn into town. There weren't many women, if any, doing all of that, and LeOra did it happily.

More important, John and LeOra loved each other deeply through their six decades of marriage. To this day, people still talk about how strong their relationship was, so much so that my grandma died on the first wedding anniversary after my grandfather's death. Still in great shape, she had vacuumed the house, gone to coffee with friends, and then told them she was going home to mow the lawn. There was a flat tire on the lawnmower, and apparently when she bent over to plug in the air pump to fill the tire, she had a massive heart attack and died before she hit the ground. On the way down, she got a deep cut on the pedal of the mower but it didn't bleed, which is how the medical examiner could tell she died before she fell.

In her diary earlier that morning, my grandma had written, "Happy 63rd Anniversary, Honey. I sure do miss you." She died of a broken heart.

So this was my mother's model of marriage, and why she always said to my dad, "You're stuck with me." There were no ifs, ands, or buts about divorce. And yet, the unthinkable had happened. Because of that, it seemed to me now like anyone could get divorced.

"Oh my God," I told Justin after my parents split. "If I'd have seen this before I got married, I don't know if I would have gotten married so quickly."

When I had previously thought about my parents' marriage, it seemed like it worked for them. I knew it wasn't what I wanted exactly, but I didn't comprehend the depths of their dysfunction and unhappiness until after they divorced. It made me question not only marriage in general and how people handle things when they become difficult, but also my limited understanding of the entire dynamic and nature of that relationship in general—including my own.

"We're not like them," Justin assured me, pointing out some of the main differences between my folks and us, like the fact that we communicated all the time. And that we often analyzed the other marriages around us: what we wanted for us, and what we didn't.

A lot of people have a hard time talking to each other about the important, deeper aspects of their relationship. If you're not open to revealing yourself to your partner and in turn listening to your partner's revelations, it can spell doom. For those of us who aren't naturally comfortable with it, trained professionals can guide us through the process.

Comfort isn't an issue with Justin and me. Justin was right; we do communicate. We talk about reality as a way to manage it, and in this moment of our lives, divorce, as ugly as it can be, was the subject matter that we were discussing. All we needed to do was sit down and be direct with each other—and that's exactly what we did.

We had nonstop conversations. We started at our anniversary dinner and we didn't stop. We started with what each of us wanted—no holds barred. We talked about all this not because we are masochists or because we wanted to get divorced. We did it because we *didn't* want to get divorced. Rather than sweep the difficulties of our long-distance relationship under the rug by ignoring them or pretending that they didn't exist, we chose to speak plainly about how to work through them and solve our issues. I'm blessed to have a husband who is deeply in touch with his own emotions and totally unafraid to confront mine. There are not many men who could do what he did. I know how lucky I am.

The turning point for me came one morning after a weeklong conversation. I woke up, looked at him, and said, "We're going to be married forever. You are my partner. You are my husband. You are my everything. I don't want to be with anybody else. And I don't want to have to have this conversation ever again. This is it."

I realized that the topic was entering into our lives because of my parents' divorce. I was deeply emotionally invested in the state of their marriage and its stability. I realized that the dynamic between my parents affected me very much as a child—my dad's absences, our moves, the ways in which my mom tried to smooth over his biting remarks—clearly there had been tension between them and much of her work was to compensate for him. What was happening to my parents occupied my thoughts day and night during the months I watched their marriage dissolve before my eyes. It took up a lot of real estate in my mind, which began to spill over into the peace and calm of my own marriage. Finally, I chose to reject those outside influences and see my relationship for what it is: healthy, good, pure, and successful independent of the fate of the relationships surrounding ours.

Still, the more important change between us happened internally. By having all those scary conversations, we plumbed the depths of how to be married *and* happy. We figured out a system that's just for ourselves and explored a full range of experiences. Although those talks were at times painful, in the end there was so much freedom in letting ourselves go there.

Having gone through that together, I can honestly say I've never been more in love with Justin. I'm so grateful for him. I'm grateful that if I bring up a negative feeling or a thought about our relationship, he won't think it's the end. He's not threatened. He's not insecure. And, thanks to him, I've become the same way. There are no games, no reading between the lines. It is direct conversation. You might cry. You might feel like crap for a little while afterward. But there are no secrets.

That's important, because at the end of the day—a long day where I've been at a crazy photo shoot and Justin's been shooting a crazy television show—all we have is each other. I can't imagine what it's going to be like when we hit our thirty-year anniversary. We'll know one another so well, in and out—wait. What am I talking about? We already finish each other's sentences. We don't need thirty years.

If our fifth wedding anniversary was a dark affair, our sixth-year anniversary dinner was the opposite. As usual, Justin made the reservation. It was at Marea, a seafood restaurant on Central Park South. I had never heard of it before, but the moment I walked in I could tell we were somewhere really glam. We passed by the warm, glowing bar of amber into the dining room decorated with conch shells dipped in silver. There was the young, gorgeous model with the octogenarian, titans of industry in their dark suits, and formal waiters pushing glass-covered trolleys with crushed ice and caviar.

"Wow," I said to Justin as we settled into our sumptuous leather chairs with a view through large plate-glass windows of the streetlights twinkling against the dark of Central Park. "How did you find this place?"

"The Internet," he said.

I burst out laughing. This anniversary was an evening filled with words of affirmation, declarations of love and affection, and positive thoughts of our future that sprang from the hope of what was still yet to come. We didn't stop laughing or talking the whole evening—and I'm confident that we never will.

chapter 9

Turning the Competition into Community

Rivalry, jealousy, and cattiness are the worst things we women do to each other. Getting over it and getting together is the key to success for all of us.

I was relaxing by the pool in Miami in the summer of 2013 when my cell phone rang. It was one of my agents, so, although I was on vacation, I picked up.

"Ashley, I wanted to let you know the whole plus-size division at Ford in New York is being shut down."

"What? I don't get it. What are you saying?"

"They are completely closing plus-size, kids, and hair and makeup. All that's left is high-end fashion."

The news came as a huge shock to me. The plus-size division in New York (the company had offices in Chicago, LA, and Miami, but New York's was the biggest) was the second-largest moneymaking division at Ford, second only to the straight-size models, and we were about half the size of the high-end fashion division. The decision to shut down all these different divisions was also perplexing, since Ford was always known for the everyday, relatable, girl-next-door models you see in catalogs, as opposed to the high-end fashion editorial models. But more than this, the idea that the agency that had been my home for the last decade was no longer representing me was terrifying. What was this going to mean for me?

After returning to New York, my fears intensified. Word spread quickly that Ford New York was dissolving its plus-size department, and our clients were freaking out. I could still technically be booked out of Ford's offices in other cities, but the agents there didn't have relationships with my clients, and I was getting texts from clients trying to book me directly. It was overwhelming, like the world had been turned on its head.

A lot of my peers, just as frightened as me, quickly signed with various other agencies. They wanted to be under a new umbrella as fast as they could, and I didn't blame them. But when two of my long-standing agents from Ford, who decided to start their own agency, sent me a contract to sign with them, I didn't jump right away.

Instead, when the upheaval began, I reached out to other models, veterans of the industry, to ask about how they did business. What I learned opened my eyes. I had been under the illusion that there is an industry standard for contracts. Now I found out that there was nothing to stop you from negotiating the contract offered when you are approached by a modeling agency.

Of course, a model only has standing if she has a name. I was lucky. At twenty-five years old, I was starting to develop a name for myself. I wasn't superfamous (I hadn't yet been in *Sports Illustrated* or on any covers; I didn't have any standing contracts), but I had my lingerie line with Addition Elle. And I had been one of the highest earners at Ford. If you booked me, I could give you fifty shots in a day, no fuss, no muss. I sold clothes. I have always had a very good reputation for working hard.

No one knew that better than my longtime agents, who were pushing me to sign with their new agency. But I wasn't ready.

"Why wouldn't you sign this contract?" one of the agents said. "I did everything for you. I made you. I started you when nobody believed in you."

He was right to a degree. Now twenty-five years old,

I had been with this man since I was fifteen. He was more than a mentor. I always did what he said, when he said it. He had never given me bad advice. By not immediately putting pen to paper and joining his agency, I felt like I was defying my father.

I had been married to Justin for three years at that point, and the soul searching we did together made me question what I wanted for myself in my career. I had come a long way from the early days of our marriage, when Justin would return home from a full day of work and grad school classes to find me in the same position he'd left me on the couch that morning. (At that point in my career, I worked on average two to three days a week.)

"What are you doing with your life?" he asked.

"I'm relaxing," I said.

That wasn't good enough for him. He was trying to push me toward having an ambition beyond merely going to work. "What do you want out of your career? Find your passion and go get it. Don't just sit there on the couch watching trash TV." (Granted, Justin also told me, "If you worked at Mc-Donald's or cleaned houses, I would love you just as much. But I want you to find meaning in your work, whatever it is.")

Those kinds of conversations opened up my eyes to look past my next booked modeling job. What did I want for my long-term future? At twenty-five, my career could be over in the next few years. What did I want to achieve before it was over? What did I want my work to stand for?

It was a brutal time, trying to figure out what was right for me while my longtime agent continued to push me to sign with him and his new agency. It wasn't pretty. Although we had been together for a long time, I was beginning to question whether he was willing or able to support the vision I had for myself. I didn't need to tell him what I wanted. He already knew. And my skepticism grew as I asked myself, if you can't do it in ten years, when are you going to be able to do it?

The whole situation gave me so much anxiety, what I really needed was a therapist. Instead I turned to my new lawyer, a great woman whom I met through Justin. She was an entertainment lawyer, and I wanted to work with her so she could protect me no matter who I signed with. Anytime my old agent would call me, I'd call her in turn. "I'm freaking out right now," I said to her. "What do I do?"

I felt rudderless and unsure of myself. Something in my gut was telling me not to jump into a new agreement with my old management, but I didn't know what the alternative might be. The industry seemed to be changing. People were more receptive to body positivity and inclusivity of all shapes and sizes. There was also a shift in the kinds of jobs available to plus-size models, as well as how much they paid. Rates for online retailers were going down (they started cutting the faces off models so they could book models with lower rates). At the same time, major catalogs and department stores were finally including big girls in their advertising—but typically only one model. The examples of the veteran curvy models who came before me weren't much help in this new landscape. I needed to find others in my situation.

One day, Inga Eiriksdottir, a curvy model from Ford whom I was friendly with but not particularly close, called me to ask the very question I had been torn over. "What are you going to do? Are you going to sign?" she asked.

When I told her I wasn't sure, she said, "Let's hang out and talk about it."

I was surprised when I got to the meetup to see Marquita Pring, a really good friend of mine, and two other plus-size models, Danielle Redman and Julie Henderson. The five of us immediately began talking about the thoughts, fears, and hopes we all shared but had bottled up. It was an incredible relief to know that there were other strong women who felt the same way I did about the situation we were in.

We met a few more times before Inga brought a brand strategist into our little group for a consultation. At first we were wary of including an outsider, someone who didn't know our industry particularly well. But sometimes an outside opinion is exactly what you need to move forward.

"You guys are in the best position of your lives," said the strategist.

"We are?" someone said, echoing the sentiments all of us had. We thought just the opposite.

"Yes. You can have anything you want."

We all sat stunned. But we knew we wanted to hear more.

"You guys are in the best position of your lives," she said again. "You should be pitching yourselves to every agency out there, and then asking these agencies for a percentage of the business that you bring them."

This was *not* how things were done, and it was hard to imagine ourselves—a few curvy models—having the power to demand money from the same folks who usually took money from us. But the strategist convinced us that we were much stronger together than as individuals. If we presented ourselves as a package deal, we represented a lot of business, and money, for any modeling agency.

The strategist then went off and did her market research, returning with a cool-looking portfolio filled with charts, graphs, written analyses, and our most beautiful images. It detailed where this segment of the fashion industry had been, where it was going, how much money was at stake, how much money each of us had made in the last year, and finally, how much money we stood to make in this growing market. It was a pretty bold move to reveal our salaries to one another. It wasn't about how much we made individually. We all put in our numbers to show agencies how much we were worth, but we didn't discuss it. We just knew who was who and that was that. It didn't make us competitive—because we were smart enough to know that if we became competitive, we'd only hurt ourselves. When you looked at us as a collective, we really were a force to be reckoned with.

As we excitedly looked through this amazing document, it dawned on each of us that we were now more than just friends and colleagues. By this point, we had all become very, very close. The entire experience was an emotional roller coaster. We were all working, but it was difficult. All of the former New York Ford plus-size models (which included all the women in our group) were booking their jobs through one agent out of Ford Chicago, and she was overwhelmed by about thirty very busy girls who had fallen into her lap. It was a lot of stress for everyone.

We models had relied on each other as support throughout. And underneath was another layer to our initiative—to make real change in the curve category. In that way, we were like a coalition. And every good coalition needs a name.

There were the obvious choices, like Curvy Girls or Plus-Size Beauty Queens. We didn't know what we wanted to be called, but we definitely didn't want to be called anything like *that*. We didn't want to be stereotypical, and we wanted to be a little edgy. If we were going to change the category, we wanted to present ourselves in a way that we had never been presented before. We wanted to push away the terms *plus-size* and *curvy*. Then Inga offered up the Icelandic word *alda*. The word had a nice sound, and its meaning, "wave," resonated. The wave could refer to the waves that the curves of our bodies made, or how we were making a wave in the fashion industry. "Alda—Alda!" we chanted.

Our coalition now official, together we made the rounds to all the biggest modeling agencies. Models and power brokers in the industry were a little confused. "Are you an agency? What are you guys doing?" No. We weren't an agency. We were a group of models with a greater mission. Some might have been confused, but everybody was watching us.

With the bible in hand that the strategist had prepared for us, we went to Muse and Wilhelmina, the only major agencies with strong plus-size divisions, and to the new agency started by our former Ford agents. But we didn't limit ourselves to the obvious places. We also had meetings with agencies that had never represented a curvy model before. The reactions to our pitch varied wildly. Some people told us no right away. "We have never even considered representing plus-size, and we're not ever going to," one agent said. That response didn't bring us down. It pushed us to go out and find an agency that would take us. Knowing exactly how much money we could bring in, we had the attitude that it was their loss.

Meanwhile, balancing things out a bit, some agencies offered us more than we could ever have imagined. There was an agency that offered us 50 percent of the 20 percent management fees for any additional plus-size model we brought into the agency.

Finally we landed a meeting at IMG, which has a huge roster of famous straight-size models—Gisele Bündchen, Karlie Kloss, Joan Smalls, the Hadid sisters (Gigi and Bella), Kate Moss, and on and on. Justin strongly suggested that I pursue IMG. They were massive; they were intimidating; they were the pinnacle. The international agency's reputation preceded itself. It was known for brand building, creating stars, landing high-end fashion spreads, and making money. But it only had one plus-size model among its ranks.

"They are exactly where you need to be!" he said. "Push for a meeting."

IMG is the best of the best. When you walk into a

room and say you are an IMG girl, you command automatic respect . . . and that's where every single member of ALDA signed!

It wasn't just an emotional decision that led us to sign our contracts but a strategic one as well. There was power in numbers at the negotiating table—and beyond. If Macy's or JCPenney calls an agency looking for a plus-size model, they aren't looking for just one model. They want to know everyone who is there. The more robust an agency's roster, the more calls it is going to get. We fought for what we wanted, and in December 2013, when we signed with IMG, we got what we wanted.

As soon as the news got out, the plus-size fashion industry was on fire. *All these models signed at IMG? What is going on?* Even more shocking was that our new agency didn't make us a separate division. The agency's president, Ivan Bart, wanted to make a statement that we were models along with and just like everyone else at IMG. That had never been done before. We had always been marginalized. It was a huge statement, and exactly what we had hoped would happen.

There was article after article about how our group was signed to IMG's regular roster, which was great publicity for all of us. This also signaled the start of a new revolution that needed to happen in the fashion world, where women with different kinds of bodies are no longer just a token—but part of the industry at large.

You'd think we would have been popping champagne corks the day we officially joined IMG, right? Wrong. I was bawling before the meeting to sign my contract with IMG, crying so hard that Justin was concerned.

"Are you okay?" he asked.

"Oh my God. I'm freaking out!"

"Why are you crying?"

"I don't know. It's a new chapter. I'm afraid that they don't know how they're going to book me, because they've never booked a plus-size model before."

While my new contract with IMG was more than I could have ever hoped for, and though they treated us throughout the negotiations with the utmost respect, what was going to happen next was a big question mark. Like getting married or giving birth, the celebratory moment was just the beginning of an unknown journey.

In my life, I never read my Bible as much as I did during my first six months at IMG. In an effort to quell my anxiety, I constantly reminded myself that God had a plan for me, that everything happens for a reason. Meanwhile, I had cause for concern. I wasn't really working that much, other than with the steady clients I had brought with me into my new relationship with IMG. It was hard for me not to hear the voices of my old agents from Ford saying, "We told you so."

Finally, during New York Fashion Week in September 2014, I couldn't take it anymore. I called a meeting with all of my agents. Even though Fashion Week is by far their busiest time of the year (they don't stop working the entire week, starting each day at 6 a.m. and finishing at midnight), they agreed and found a time to meet with me on Saturday morning. The fact that I called an emergency meeting with all of them was a very big deal.

"I'm really not happy. I have not even made half as much money as I made last year," I said. "I want to work *every single day.*"

"The first year at a new agency is always the hardest," one of IMG's reps said. "We're learning you. You're learning us."

They knew I was a star, they said. It was just a matter of time, offering up the example of Heidi Klum, who had been a catalog girl and was contemplating starting a luggage line when all of a sudden *Project Runway* fell in her lap.

"Your time is coming," another agent said.

I couldn't say that IMG hadn't been trying. The first Fashion Week after I signed with the agency, back in February of that year, they set me up on twenty castings a day. That took a lot of guts on their part to break the plus-size barrier and send me into rooms filled with straight-size models and designers who had never considered curves on their runway. It took even more guts on my part to go into those rooms with confidence.

Honestly, though, it sucked. I was always the biggest girl by far during that week of castings. Everyone was looking at me, wondering why I was there. In my head I imagined they thought I was lost or with the catering crew.

I wore black, head to toe, always. My theory—black is not only chic but also slimming. Entering castings with people who had never booked a plus-size model, the last thing I wanted to do was overwhelm them with hips, thighs, and breasts. As a curvy pioneer, I had to go slow, so I wore a classic black tank top and black ripped jeans. Cool but understated. The model's uniform. Of course, I also wore a heel, because when you're going out on runway shows, you need to show you can walk in a heel. I don't know if I have the best walk in the world, but I know that I'm confident.

I was also confident while waiting around in a room filled with very, very thin models—or at least I projected confidence, no matter how I felt inside. Straight-size models are notoriously quiet and don't talk to each other in castings, generally because many are very young or from other countries and often not comfortable speaking English. But I was no straight-size model, so I broke the silence. I said hi to anyone who made eye contact. Every girl offered back a friendly hi. Then I'd strike up a conversation.

"What agency are you with?"

"Marilyn. You?"

"IMG."

"You're with IMG?"

"Yeah, I'm with IMG."

"Oh."

The confusion stemmed from the fact that IMG is probably the number one modeling agency in the world, and I'm fat. (At least in this world.) That was always a fun moment. I wasn't trying to psych anyone out so that I could get her job. A ninety-five-pound Russian model and I are not in direct competition. It was just my subtle way of saying that I had as much a right to be in that room as anyone else.

Despite my bravado and all-black ensembles, I didn't

get booked for anything that week. I wasn't surprised, but it was still a disappointment.

But I did get in front of the casting directors of *Harper's Bazaar.* And just like my agents at IMG promised, my time did come. I was booked for Carine Roitfeld's first beauty editorial for *Harper's*—something I never, *ever* thought could happen to me. The former editor-in-chief of *Vogue Paris* and epitome of chic assembled a group of big-name models that included Carolyn Murphy, Ashleigh Good, Riley Montana, and me. It wasn't a special shape issue, just a straight-up, high-end fashion editorial. "Wow, you're an incredible model," Carine told me, which, in my opinion, is fashion's version of being knighted, because she is one of the most renowned voices in fashion.

From the *Harper's* launchpad, I got an editorial in the biannual British style magazine *Love,* then in quick succession four covers of English magazines—that's four more covers than I ever had at my former agency. I'm not sure why my first cover success was in England. Whether because British lawmakers have banned certain airbrushed ads (and one department store put a ban on retouched images of models in lingerie) or that they seem to have more brands with extended sizes, I have always felt they are more accepting of body diversity in the UK. (I even told one of my sisters, a curvy girl like me, to go there to try to find a husband. She wound up saving herself the cost of a plane ticket by snagging her hubby in Nebraska.)

The rest is history—from *Cosmo* to *Maxim* to *Elle* to *Self* to *Glamour* and more, I turned into the cover girl I never thought I was. What's really interesting about my story, though, isn't just that I, as a curvy woman, broke through a barrier in my industry. It's also that I could never have done it alone. If I hadn't banded together with the other women in ALDA, my career would not be where it is today.

We broke through another barrier when we formed our coalition, because the modeling industry (like so many other industries, but even more so) is set up for you to hate your competition. Those are the other girls that "get your job" and make you feel like a failure in the ultimate goal to see who can be the most famous, who can be the most recognizable, who can make the most money. Because any model can be your rival, we were taught not to talk to each other about our ambitions, drives, and especially not money. Through ALDA we realized that talking about business gave us infor-mation—and power.

Women have to support each other more. *Women get women.* We understand each other when we are happy or sad, when we have our period, start a new job, or fall in love. We are typically the caretakers. Let's take care of each other, start building each other up. The stereotype with women is that we are catty and vindictive. It's important to fight against that notion. I have a no-BS policy in my circle. If I find a woman is tearing down me or anyone else I know, that's a deal breaker.

I grew so much as an individual, and it was because I had the support of my colleagues. I love those girls. Psy-chologically, I couldn't have gotten out of my ten-year rela-tionship with my former agency without the support of the women of ALDA. We had three-hour-long meetings once a week that were so intense they were like group therapy. In those meetings, I felt like I had to be the hard, strong one. "We have to do what's right for us!" I said, like a regular Norma Rae. But I also cried all the time. It was just fear, on fear, on fear.

Without them, I would not have had that portfolio showcasing our strength and outlining our demands. I would not have gotten out of my complicated relationship with my former agents, and my career certainly would have plateaued.

The key to the whole thing was never viewing these women as my competition, which would have been natural, since in some senses they *were* my competition. It helped that we were all confident people and making good money, but once we started meeting regularly, it was impossible to think of these ladies as anything other than sisters-in-arms. One of us was delegated to emails, one organized the meeting place and made sure everyone knew it, one got all the snacks for the meeting, and one made all the calls. The more we worked together, the stronger we felt.

These women allowed me to take that leap of faith and overcome the anxiety I had over the unknown. Without that, I'm 100 percent sure I wouldn't be where I am today, working every day, the way I wanted to be. The way my agents at IMG said I would.

As for the other women of ALDA, I'm so proud of them and what they have achieved. To this day we all still talk. "What are you doing?" "What do you want?" "How are you getting there?" We are still asking the same questions as when we first started meeting, and always encouraging one another.

That's why I always say: When models talk there will be trouble—for those trying to stand in our way. The same goes for all strong women. Trust me.

Postscript
Beauty Beyond Size

In March 2017, I made history. For the first time ever, American *Vogue* put a plus-size model on its cover when I appeared alongside Gigi Hadid, Kendall Jenner, Adwoa Aboah, Liu Wen, Vittoria Ceretti, and Imaan Hammam.

The concept behind the cover, shot by the famous fashion photography couple Inez van Lamsweerde and Vinoodh Matadin, was to highlight how diverse modeling has become. Models are no longer just the typical runway variety; we come in all kinds of ethnicities and body shapes. We have all kinds of backgrounds and aspirations. We are activists, athletes, and leaders.

For the shoot, everyone was dressed in Prada, which custom-made me a cute knit skort and thin knit turtleneck. All the girls had matching outfits with different-colored bottoms and funky belts. I felt amazing that Prada had made an outfit especially for my size—and even better that the bottoms were too big. You can always take a garment in to make it more form-fitting, but when it's too small, you just feel fat.

We were on the beach in Malibu, the sun shining and the water sparkling, when Inez and Vinoodh lined us all up so that we could hold each other for the iconic *Vogue* cover that testified we are the supermodels of today.

It's hard to put into words what this moment means to me. *Vogue* puts an article about an important curvy woman in their pages once in a while and the occasional curvy celebrity on its cover, but never a model like me. The impact on the fashion industry can't be overstated; if American *Vogue* gives something its blessing, it becomes the industry standard.

The whole thing is even more amazing considering that the first time I met Anna Wintour—*Vogue's* longtime editor-in-chief, artistic director for publisher Condé Nast, and basically the ruler of the fashion universe—it was a fiasco.

The occasion was the LA premiere, held in April of 2016, of the documentary *First Monday in May*. Named for the date of the 2015 Met Gala, the film offers a behind-the-scenes view of the annual party that has been called fashion's Super Bowl and the corresponding exhibition at the museum's Costume Institute. Both are firmly under Anna Wintour's direction.

In the media, Wintour has a reputation for being cold, even steely. The book and film *The Devil Wears Prada* is supposedly based on her, but peers have told me she is actually kind, just a woman with a massive amount of responsibility. Still, I was crazy intimidated when I spotted her in a soft sundress that evening in LA. Although she was clearly open to receiving people who wanted to come by and say hello, or to congratulate her on the beautiful film, I felt like it could ruin my future in the fashion industry if I breathed on her wrong.

Designer Rachel Roy, also at the event, encouraged me to introduce myself to the editor-in-chief. "This is your chance," she said. I trust Rachel, who is a business mentor to me, so I took Justin's hand and said, "We are going to meet Anna Wintour and then walk away. Be cool, and we'll be fine."

As we approached, Justin was really excited because he knew how important this was for me. Anna could easily change a model's career. If she thinks you're good, it opens the door to appearing in a lot of Condé Nast publications, which are some of the most important in the fashion industry. That, in turn, leads to more designers wanting to dress you, which can then lead to lucrative hair and makeup contracts, etc.

I introduced Justin and myself. She greeted us politely. Then, out of the blue, my husband said, "Hi, Anna! I just have to give you a hug."

What?!

I don't care how kind she is in real life; you *do not* hug Anna Wintour at a public event. It was like I was watching a car accident in slow motion as Justin leaned in and put his arms around her. All I saw were her two little forearms come around and pat his back. "Nice to meet you," she said quietly, then took a step back.

"I'm so sorry," I said. "Nice to meet you. Good-bye."

I took Justin's arm like he was a child about to get into some serious trouble. I was fuming.

"Oh my God, do you know what you just did?" I whispered-screamed at him in a corner.

He was sorry. He was trying to act normal—and we are a hugging kind of people. Justin felt terrible, because he loves me and would bend over backward to help me achieve whatever I want in my career. There was nothing for me to do at this point but pretend like it had never happened, even though it *so* happened.

Not long after, my agent Mina called to tell me that I was on hold to attend the Met Gala! This is one of the most coveted invitations in the industry. You have to be chosen by Anna Wintour and/or a designer to attend. Mina let me know I had been approved by *Vogue* but that I still didn't have a designer to dress me or a confirmed seat.

Well, I didn't go to the Costume Institute's gala that year.

"I don't know what happened," Mina told me a week or so later, "but all the leads I had for designers fell through."

I knew exactly what happened, or at least I thought I did in that moment of panic and disappointment. I told Justin, "It's because you hugged Anna Wintour!"

Of course, looking back, I know now it probably wasn't Justin's fault (sorry, honey). It honestly might have been that there just wasn't a designer to dress me. I will never really know. All I know is that, like most curvy women, sometimes I have a hard time finding clothes that fit.

Case in point, my first *Vogue* cover, which wasn't for the American magazine. I was on the cover of the UK edition's January 2017 issue. British *Vogue* had never featured a plus-size model on the cover, but then editor-in-chief Alexandra

Shulman has been at the forefront on body diversity issues, and she got really fierce about discrimination against bigger women in fashion in the editor's letter she wrote for my cover issue.

"The shoot was put together fairly last-minute and we are all very grateful to the people at Coach who, under the creative direction of Stuart Vevers, moved speedily to provide clothes for us that had to come from outside their sample range," Alexandra wrote. "They were enthusiastic about dressing a woman who is not a standard model, but sadly there were other houses that flatly refused to lend us their clothes. It seems strange to me that while the rest of the world is desperate for fashion to embrace broader definitions of physical beauty, some of our most famous fashion brands appear to be travelling in the opposite—and, in my opinion, unwise—direction."

I had no idea about any of this when I did the *Vogue* shoot with Patrick Demarchelier. I felt confident in his hands because I had worked with him for a *Glamour Magazine* shoot and he is the consummate professional. Working with a small crew, he takes only ten to fifty pictures per outfit, whereas some photographers take a couple hundred shots. Because of his depth of experience and artistry, he doesn't need to do more.

My look for the British *Vogue* shoot, held in Brooklyn's Coney Island, was '90s supermodel, with barely there makeup; tousled, dry, wavy hair with no extensions; light, washed denim Levi's; and tucked-in white T-shirts with an oversize leather jacket from Coach cropped at the hip. Patrick had me furrowing my brow a lot to give the impression of an intense, sexy chick who is sure of herself.

On the set, I was going crazy. This was my first *Vogue* cover! (Maybe. You never know if you'll actually be the cover until it's confirmed, not long before the issue actually comes out.) But all the people surrounding me—hair, makeup, and styling—were veterans with many *Vogue* covers under their belts. They all had the same message: "Girl, get used to it; this is your new norm." That was their way of saying they believed in me. Although I was older than most models and a lot bigger, they saw that there was so much more to come.

It was hard for me to believe. Despite all my confidence and success, I never, ever, *ever* thought I would be *Vogue* cover girl material. Considering that the magazine had such a hard time finding designers to lend me clothes, I wasn't wrong to think the odds were against me. And even now I ask myself, if I were a model in image alone and didn't have a voice, would I be on the cover? I'm not so sure.

But I do have a voice. In the last few years, I've become an icon for curvy women, an example of how to be big and beautiful. In 2016 I was named *Glamour* Woman of the Year for being a "body activist." In 2015 I was called on to be a true expert in my field when I gave my very first TEDx Talk, "Plus-Size? More Like My Size." Around the same time, *Forbes* named me to its prestigious 30 Under 30 Art & Style list.

All these accolades and opportunities have come about, not because I landed an H&M campaign or have my own lingerie line, but because I was willing to reveal, celebrate even, that which so much of media, my industry, and society put down. Here I am, talking about my thick thighs, cellulite, less-than-upstanding breasts, and serious butt in interviews, on social media, anywhere I am given the chance.

I put myself out there, trying to prove that beauty is beyond size. It was risky, sure, but what I risked in terms of personal pride was nothing in comparison to what I was rewarded in terms of personal fulfillment. It is very similar to what happened when I bonded with my peers to create ALDA, which is where the phrase Beauty Beyond Size was born. (At least as far as I'm concerned.)

In the portfolio we created to pitch to agencies one of the sections was named Beauty Beyond Size. I love that phrase. Believe me, if there's a pun or play on words around body size, I've heard it—and frankly I'm sick of all of them. It seems that anytime someone writes an article about bigger women, the title is along the lines of "Ahead of the Curve" or "Danger, Curves Ahead." If I never see either of those again, it'll be too soon.

When I saw Beauty Beyond Size, it felt fresh and amazingly meaningful. Your size does not define your beauty— and in that way, the message goes beyond your body measurements to be a metaphor for all other meaningless and superficial limitations.

Then I did what we all do now when we find a word or a phrase we connect with; I hashtagged it on Instagram. There is nothing new under the sun—or on the Internet— but when women saw me posting #beautybeyondsize, showing less-than-perfect behind-the-scenes pictures from my photo shoots or cellulite selfies, I like to think I started a movement.

The Internet is a funny place, because it's a forum for so many awful ideas, body shaming, bullying, and the like. The negative side of social media is that everybody thinks they're experts with the right to weigh in on whether you are healthy, beautiful, a positive voice for the plus-size community—or not. I have experienced backlash from so many different pictures over the years. Sometimes I'm called too fat, sometimes too skinny. Gross, exhibitionist, dangerous. You name the judgmental adjective and I've been called it.

Yet, at the same time, the Internet is a place where women can find solidarity, no matter who or where they are. By seeing the images others have put up of their back fat or stretch marks, women are able to connect with their tribe, those who they never met but who look like them, curvy ladies who, by posing in their lingerie and swimsuits, are saying, "So what? I've got my tiger stripes, and so do you."

These are definitely my girls.

I also owe a special debt of gratitude toward women of color for whom my body type, as a standard of beauty, is not unique. For many black and brown people, curves have long been desirable. As my relationship with Justin has helped me understand, one of the aspects of our country's shameful history of racial injustice is that women of color have had their natural bodies stigmatized as overtly sexual or shunned as ugly because they don't fit into a traditional European standard of beauty. I'm fully aware that I'm being praised for something a lot of women of color have been put down for, simply because I'm white. I hope that my work will help break down all the barriers we put up around other people—whether it's because of their body type, skin color, or any other external trait.

Naturally, my focus is within the plus-size fashion community, where we have had our own set of rules for beauty. Up until very recently in catalogs, advertisements, and the occasional curvy issue of a magazine, the only kind of girl represented has been one that looks like me: hourglass figure, pretty face, brunette or blonde. As a plus-size model, that's our job, to be this picture-perfect, plump, beautiful woman, with a flat stomach and a skinny face, who wears size 18 max, and probably 14 or 16. But for the plus-size customer—whether it's a woman who gained a lot of weight after having children or the one who's been a big girl all her life—images of models like me might feel just as unattainable as the proportions of a Victoria's Secret model do to a thinner woman.

I believe fashion should be aspirational. Seeing a gorgeous plus-size model wearing a holiday dress in a catalog can inspire you to glam yourself up or give you new ideas on your style. But there's also a place for reality. I'm talking about the size-22 woman, or the girl who's five-one with very small breasts and a large stomach. When they all started coming out and posting #beautybeyondsize, it was a way for women to see themselves through other women's eyes (as opposed to the eyes of marketers and editors). The Instagram page under that hashtag has become a safe place where you can find a woman who looks like you as well as confident and gorgeous role models who aren't famous.

The community that has risen up around that hashtag is nothing short of inspirational. Each of the 136,611 posts (as of March 2017) brings something amazingly unique to the conversation. I urge you to go and see, and if you are inspired, post for yourself.

Heck, there is a paparazzi picture of me wearing a see-through, body-clinging, polka-dot dress that shows my every ripple, curve, and crease.

Social media is just a jumping-off point. I want my voice to be louder than a picture of my cellulite on Twitter with a caption that reads, "Love who you are." I'm in a position now—thanks to the hundreds of thousands of women who have put me there—to speak to my industry and demand better treatment for those of us who have hated our bodies because we weren't properly represented. I am standing up to demand that we feel better about ourselves.

In this revolution, the quiet moments are just as powerful as the loud ones. My mom received a letter from a student at the high school where she works in Nebraska. In the letter, the senior detailed how she was always the big girl and never wore jeans because she always felt fat. Because of her size, she also never felt as good as her friends. Then, on Instagram, she came across a plus-size model in her underwear and the image was life changing. To see someone really, truly big, wearing gorgeous lingerie with pleasure, out on social media for the world to see, well . . .

The senior knew who I was even before she realized my mom worked at the school. When she found out, though, she wrote a heartfelt, eloquent letter to my mom, where she said, "Thank you for raising Ashley." When I came home to visit, my mom arranged for the three of us to have coffee, and we talked about all the stuff you'd imagine we would. What was remarkable about that afternoon was to witness my mother as she heard this conversation. She had never had this experience before.

"When I'm with you, I see the difference you're making in people's lives," my mom told me. "And it's not because you're pretty; it's because you are making other people feel okay with who they are. That's what's important. Beauty doesn't last, but how you made those people feel will.

"I did something right," she told me.

To hear those words from my mother was more meaningful than any award could ever be.

I've always been told to "enjoy it now because it won't last forever"—and not just by my mother. Agents, other models, they all told me to enjoy the travel, the money, being in the public eye—because one day it will all be over. Perhaps an example from the modeling world is a more extreme version of it, but this message is hammered home to all women.

The heart of my power is not my beauty but my willingness to explore my deepest vulnerabilities with others, to talk about the same issues every other woman has, in an open and honest way. No matter how many stylists or makeup artists or personal trainers I have helping me look my best, I, too, battle insecurity, frustration, judgment, and feeling ugly.

When I modeled in my second lingerie fashion show during New York Fashion Week, I was having one of those very days. Right before I got on the runway, in nothing but panties and a bra, looking like the epitome of self-assurance, I was anything but. Why? Because I didn't believe in the quality of my lingerie line? Nope. The fashion show was disorganized? No. The other girls walking didn't look their best? Not that either. No, it was that stupid thing that so many of us women do to ourselves: I felt like I was bigger than I was the year before.

As soon as I hit the runway, I actively changed my thinking. Even if it wasn't exactly going to be an ego booster to see my cellulite all over the Internet and Instagram, I knew I had to look beyond that in my mind and know that I was using my body to change someone's life.

I was given a voice, not just to feel great in my skin but so that you can feel great in *your* skin.

Listen up: do you have uneven fat on your thighs, cellulite on your upper arms? Do you have to wear double Spanx and a DDD bra? You are not alone. So do I. When I put myself out there, flaws and all, that's the moment I realized I was more than just a pretty face.

It's in this spirit that I wrote this book, which I hope will help close the chapter on the social preoccupation with the external. No matter how beautiful—or not—one is perceived to be, the true beauty we all possess is found on the inside. That should be our focus and the measure by which we are judged. How do we move through life? What other lives have we touched? Who have we confronted with love? How have we changed the world for the better? Those are all qualities that can't be counted or weighed. Really, beauty beyond size.

Acknowledgments

First and foremost, thank you to my mother. Mom, you've always been the most important woman in my life. Thank you for instilling values in me; for making me feel beautiful, confident, and brave; and for loving me unconditionally. I wouldn't be where I am today without your help and your direction since the early days of my career. Thank you to my entire family, who have supported me since day one. To my younger sisters, thank you for giving me the opportunity to be your role model.

To my agent, Mina White, one of the strongest, most hardworking women I know: I admire your drive and can never thank you enough for believing in me, elevating my career to new heights, and making possible what I thought was impossible. You're a superwoman! To Ivan Bart: Your ideas that spark change in the fashion and modeling industries and your passion for celebrating diversity inspire me every day. I'll forever be proud to be an IMG star.

To my teams of phenomenal women at WME and Skai Blue Media—Nancy Josephson, Suzanne Lyon, Andy McNicol, Rakia Reynolds, and Christanna Ciabattoni: Thank you for supporting me day in and day out, and for using your creative minds to tell my story and amplify my mission.

Thanks to Rachel Aschalew, my ride-or-die, my big sister, and the best friend a girl could ask for. And to my right-hand woman, Darsell Obregon, I'd be lost without you.

To Carrie Thornton: Your vision made this book possible, and your creativity made it work. Thanks to Rebecca Paley, the best collaborator any author could hope for. Gratitude to all the folks at Dey Street Books, including Lynn Grady, Sean Newcott, Michael Barrs, Heidi Richter, Ploy Siripant, Stephanie Vallejo, and Nyamekye Waliyaya, for putting all the pieces together and getting this book out into the world! Thank you to Cass Bird and my glam squad for the perfect book cover.

To the teams at Addition Elle, swimsuitsforall, Dressbarn, Marina Rinaldi, and Lane Bryant, and to the editors, journalists, photographers, and bloggers who've embraced the body positive movement: Thank you all for supporting my career. Together let's break down more barriers and show everyone that size is just a number . . . a sexy number!

To my husband, Justin Ervin. God blessed me with my soulmate—you are my everything and you truly complete me. Thank you for igniting my fire, for pushing me to explore opportunities that were once unimaginable, for loving me with your entire heart, and most of all, for just being you.

And last but certainly not least, thank you to my fans. In a world where not every curvy girl has a friend to relate to, to share clothes with, to talk to about her body insecurities—I'm here for you, and you're here for me. Remember to speak life into your body, because confidence is always beautiful. Never let your body hold you back. Beauty *is* beyond size!

About the Author

Ashley Graham is a model, designer, and body activist. She began her career at the age of twelve, when she was discovered in a mall in her hometown of Lincoln, Nebraska. Ashley has worked in numerous areas of the fashion industry, including editorial, catalog, runway, commercial, television, and film. In February 2016 she was selected as a *Sports Illustrated* Swimsuit Rookie and also landed one of three covers for the magazine, making her the first size 14 model to ever be featured on the cover. A leader for the body positive movement, Ashley has been featured on the covers of *Vogue*, *Vogue UK*, *Cosmopolitan*, *SELF*, *Maxim*, and many more. In November 2016 *Glamour* named her "Woman of the Year," while Mattel simultaneously created a one-of-a-kind Barbie in her likeness. She has collaborated with Canadian brand Addition Elle on her own line of seductive, size-conscious lingerie and recently launched "Beyond by Ashley Graham," an exclusive dress collection in collaboration with Dressbarn. Additionally, she works with swimsuitsforall, designing and modeling an annual swimsuit collection.

Ashley is a sought-after television personality, with guest hosting spots on numerous national talk shows and as a judge on VH1's *America's Next Top Model*. She speaks regularly at national conferences, high schools, and girls' groups about body image, self-acceptance, and female empowerment.

She lives in Brooklyn with her husband.